Last Rays of the Setting Sun

LAST RAYS *of* THE SETTING SUN

TERENCE B. FOLEY

LAST RAYS OF THE SETTING SUN
Copyright © 2015 by Terence B. Foley

All rights reserved. Printed in the United States of America.
No part of this book may be used or reproduced in any manner whatsoever without written permission except in the case of brief quotations embodied in critical articles or reviews.

Requests for permission should be addressed to:
grlreprtr@gmail.com

This book may be purchased for educational, business or sales promotional use.
For information, please visit Amazon.com.

FIRST EDITION

Edited by Amanda Bennett, Chloe Yidan Xie and Jing Chen, Ph.D.

Cover and interior designed by KS Revivo.

Library of Congress Cataloging-In-Publication has been applied for.

ISBN-979-8-9850776-1-2

TABLE OF CONTENTS

I .... Introduction
VII .... Romanization

The Poems

3 .... 龜雖壽
5 .... 蒿里行
8 .... 七步詩
11 .... 敕勒歌
14 .... 登幽州台歌
17 .... 詠柳
20 .... 登鸛鵲樓
23 .... 涼州詞
26 .... 過故人莊
30 .... 宿建德江
33 .... 春曉
36 .... 別董大
39 .... 雜詩

42	鹿柴
45	送元二使安西
48	山居秋暝
52	九月九日憶山東兄弟
55	竹里館
58	送別
61	早發白帝城
64	望廬山瀑布
68	贈汪倫
71	送友人
75	送孟浩然之廣陵
79	望天門山
82	靜夜思
85	桃花溪
88	涼州詞
92	江畔獨步尋花
95	春望
99	登高
102	前出塞
106	自京赴奉先縣
109	絕句
112	逢雪宿芙蓉山主人
115	滁州西澗
118	漁歌子

頁碼	篇名
121	塞下曲
124	塞下曲
127	游子吟
131	觀獵
134	出塞
137	芙蓉樓送辛漸
141	游春曲
144	調張籍
147	楓橋夜泊
150	雨過山村
153	望洞庭
156	烏衣巷
159	暮江吟
162	憶江南
165	草
167	憫農
170	鋤禾
173	江雪
175	尋隱者不遇
178	雁門太守行
181	題都門南莊
184	山行
187	赤壁
190	泊秦淮

193	秋夕
196	過華清宮
199	清明
202	夜雨寄北
205	雛鳳清于老鳳聲
209	樂游原
212	傷田家
215	江鷗
217	流水
219	流水
223	泊船瓜洲
227	梅花
230	春日偶成
233	題西林壁
236	飲湖上初晴後雨
239	惠崇《春江曉景》
243	絕句
246	病牛
249	曉出淨慈寺送林子方
253	小池
256	示兒
259	秋夜將曉，出籬門迎涼有感
263	游山西村
266	四時田園雜興

269	觀書有感
272	湖上
275	橫溪堂春曉
278	樵夫
281	游園不值
285	江村晚眺
287	題臨安邸
290	月子彎彎照九州
294	天淨沙・秋思
297	田舍夜春
300	詠石灰
303	由商丘入永城途中作
306	軍中夜感
309	貞溪初夏
312	雜詩
315	明日

Introduction

Translating

Classical Chinese, in contrast to modern Chinese, is a monosyllabic language that depends on word order for sense. Fortunately Chinese word order is similar to English so that if the translator does little more than decode from Chinese word-for-word, one is pleasantly surprised to find a readable translation. While this is encouraging, one has only just arrived at the point of literary discretion: the reconciliation between translation and poetry.

Chinese characters taken individually are concise and concrete. Chinese poetry is not. Translating ambiguous Chinese poetry into our Indo-European language entails imposing precision where none exists in the original—pronouns, person, tense, number. What must be retained are the important images. An ear for the patterns of sound must be developed. It is an accomplishment to translate the feeling and sound of the original; it is far more difficult to produce a translation with meter. The translator should try to give the same number of stresses in English as there are characters in Chinese. Rhyme is very difficult to reproduce. Just remember that there is no such thing as an incorrect translation. Every person who translates Chinese poetry creates a unique translation.

Development of Chinese Poetic Forms

Chinese poetry uses many of the devices we are accustomed to in Western poetry. Alliteration (*shuang sheng* 雙聲) is common. Onomatopoeia (*ni sheng* 擬聲) is also common, especially in early poetry. But our overriding concern with Chinese poetry is meter, which is shaped by the structure of the Chinese language.

Classical Chinese is monosyllabic. The fact that each character has only one syllable dictates that the meter is determined by the number of characters in a line. The meter of the earliest Chinese poetry (*shi* [*shih* 詩]) is four characters to a line.

This is the dominant form of the songs and ballads which appear in China's earliest poetry collection the *Book of Songs* (*Shi Jing* [*Shih Ching*] 詩經). Many of the songs have four lines with three verses. Ballads vary in length, running to four or six lines. But overall, the Chinese folksong meter was the four-character line. Rhyme appears at the end of the line, but may appear elsewhere. Words may rhyme initially, internally or on all four lines. In a quatrain, the second and fourth lines rhyme. Early Chinese poetry is basically syllabic, and remained so from the Han (B.C. 206–A.D. 220) to the Tang dynasties (A.D. 618–907).

A major event in prosody occurred during the Han when the four-character line began to evolve into the (pentasyllabic) five-character line. There was ample precedent for this. Five-character lines had cropped up in earlier poetry, and the writing of prose in the five-character meter was a well established literary form. But it was only toward the end of the third century that the five-character line established itself as a standard meter. Thereafter its features became set. Lines are usually end-stopped and are self-contained units, or perhaps more correctly, couplets are end-stopped. Rhyme occurs at the end of the line on alternate lines. Lines are read with a caesura between the second and third characters, giving a 2:3 rhythm. In time, parallelism came to be emphasized. Five-character poetry became the norm until seven-character (heptasyllabic) poetry emerged during the Tang Dynasty to rival it in popularity.

Developments Between the Han and Tang Dynasties

Among the important literary developments that occurred between the Han and the Tang, two in particular set the stage for the golden age of Chinese poetry: parallelism (*pian wen* 駢文) and matching tones.

Parallelism, long a feature of both old style poetry and prose, became systematized during this period. Although parallelism appears in the literature of many languages, the monosyllabic nature of Classical Chinese lends itself especially well to paired, contrasting binomes. Characters align precisely in opposition to characters in adjacent lines. Parallelism appears extensively in China's earliest literature, the pre-Qin (Ch'in) Dynasty philosophical treatises. Later, parallelism achieved great popularity during the Six Dynasties period (A.D. 220–589). The italic style (*fu* 賦) or prose-poem, a hybrid mix of prose and poetry popular from the Han, employed parallelism extensively. Parallelism continued to be popular until a reaction against it set in during the Mid-Tang. Thereafter it became marginalized, only to re-revived during the Qing (Ch'ing) Dynasty (1644–1911).

Matching the tones of Chinese characters was the second important development that took place between the Han and the Tang. The Chinese began to have an awareness of the tonality of their language, gained through translating Buddhist texts. Tones however, were naturally modulated. Through the fourth century there developed a preference for the arrangement of tones in poetry. The gifted poet-historian Shen Yue (A.D. 441-513) is credited with the "discovery" of the theory of matching tones. By his time a tangle of prohibitions and regulations had evolved governing the arrangement of tones in verse. But whatever awareness of tonal euphony had predated him, his Table of Four Tones codified rules, definitively set forth tonal distinctions, and prescribed rules for tonal sequence. From the seventh century the "new style" poetry based on tones began to co-exist with the "old style" poetry which had not concerned itself with the arrangement of tones.

Classical Chinese had four tones: level tone

Introduction

(*ping* 平), rising tone (*shang* 上), falling tone (*qu* 去), and entering tone (*ru* 入). These four tones are combined into two categories for the purpose of poesy—level and deflected. The high-level or high-rising tone constitutes its own group. The remaining tones which either rise, fall, or end abruptly in a glottal stop are collectively termed deflected.

The Tang Dynasty

The Tang Dynasty is the high point of Chinese poetry, and one of the great moments of world literature. It is also a period of immense literary output. The imperial Tang poetry collection contains nearly fifty thousand poems by twenty five hundred poets. Among its greatest poets Bai Juyi (722–846) has 2,800 poems extant, Du Fu (712–771) 2,200 and Li Bai (701–762) over 1,000. Those three are world famous, but are only three among many in an age populated by poetic geniuses.

The development of parallelism and tone-matching had paved the way for the grandeur of Tang poetry. In addition, several more features appeared which brought Tang poetry to an even high level of sophistication and made its composition demand even greater technical virtuosity: the seven-character line (*qiyan shi* 七言詩), regulated verse (*lü shi* [*lü shih*] 律詩) and the quatrain (*jue ju* [*chueh chu*] 絕句).

The Seven-character Line

The seven-character line appears as early as the Han, but only came into the mainstream during the Tang after the five-character line had reigned for four hundred years. It came to assume equal stature with the five-character line, and was written by all major Tang poets. The seven-character line generally follows the shape of the five-character line; rhyme occurs on alternate lines. The caesura is placed after the third character so that the line is read 3:4.

Lü Shi (Lü Shih) or Regulated Verse

Both five-character and seven-character lines are employed in the two major verse forms of the Tang—regulated verse (*lü shi* 律詩) and the quatrain (*jue ju* [*chueh chu*] 絕句). *Lü shi* has a length of eight lines and might be termed a Chinese sonnet. Eight-line poems were common, but had no tonal arrangement. The *lü shi* combined the two features. Strict rules of tonal sequence must be followed. In a five-character line the second and fourth characters must be of a different tone. The last three characters in a line cannot have identical tones. The eight lines are composed of four couplets, and within each couplet the second character of the first line and the second character of the second line must differ. These in turn are to be the same tone as the corresponding characters in adjacent couplets. Rhyme occurs on the second, fourth, sixth and eighth lines. The *lü shi* took the two basic tonal patterns for the couplet and alternated them through the four couplets of the poem as a fixed requirement. In some seven-character poems the first line also rhymes. The rhyme is maintained throughout the poem, and all rhyming words are voiced in the level tone. Parallelism in regulated verse applies to the two middle couplets. It was common in the third and fourth lines and necessary in lines five and six. The last two lines, numbers seven and eight, were deliberately not paralleled.

Lü shi can generally be divided into three parts. The first couplet establishes the theme and sets up our expectations; the middle couplets inform the reader of specifics; the final couplet expresses the poet's feeling. The impact of the poem depends on the final couplet, where the poet displays wit, remorse, parody or other sentiments and is intended to elicit a response from the reader.

Jue Ju (*Chueh Chu*) or Quatrain

The quatrain (*jue ju* 絕句) (also translated as "broken-off lines" or "snapped-off lines") can be either a five-character or seven-character poem, but it is only four lines long. Its form is identical to the second half of a *lü shi* and it follows some of the same rules as a *lü shi*. The tones of each couplet are alternated, level and deflected. The rhyme can be A-A-B-A or A-B-C-B. Because of its brevity, the *jue ju* does not have a series of rhymed couplets. Parallelism is not compulsory. It is optional in lines one and two but not used in lines three and four. As the *jue ju* evolved during the Tang, the first and second lines came to be complete sentences. The third and fourth lines may be complete sentences, however the third sentence may not be a complete unit and may run over to be completed in the last line. In the hands of the Tang masters the lean, compressed *jue ju* came to compete with the ancient-style poetry, and like the Japanese haiku, was compelled to accomplish as much as a longer poem in half the length by relying on the power of suggestion.

Shi continued to evolve through the Tang. Early Tang poetry was written by imperial courtiers who flattered officials at court banquets with lofty artifice. *Fu gu* poetry, the Return-to-the-Ancient style, arose to challenge the court style. The Confucian moralist Chen Zi-ang 陳子昂 (661-702) is the progenitor of the style which, in time, came to be absorbed into the High Tang style.

Shi also became popularized. During the second half of the seventh century, Tang poetry ceased to be solely the property of courtiers. Literati at all levels wrote it. People both in and out of office wrote it, and friends wrote it to friends. The subject area also broadened to include the commonplace: peasants, soldiers, firewood gatherers. Exotic elements appeared, as Central Asian civilizations exerted a cultural influence. The relationship between poet and reader became more intimate. By the end of the dynasty, Tang poetry had changed considerably, becoming dark and melancholy. Late Tang poetry is denser, more complicated, full of allusions. The poems are thick with references to earlier literature, place names and mythology, all of which imbue the poems with special associations to the Chinese reader. Late Tang poetry is also very imaginative.

This great body of poetry is difficult to analyze. The dynasty was very long, many poets composed, many styles flourished and many moods prevailed. Chinese literary critics have divided the Tang into four periods: Early Tang (618-712), High Tang (713-765), Mid-Tang (766-846), and Late Tang (847-907).

The *Ci* (*Tz'u*) or Lyric of the Song (Sung) Dynasty

The Lyric of the Song Dynasty (*ci* 詞) became the verse style associated with the Song Dynasty (960-1279). The poetic forms which had preceded the *ci* are termed *shi* 詩 and are characterized by a regular meter. The *ci* is not a type of *shi*, and has lines of varying length. The *shi*, *ci* and the Yuan Dynasty *qu* (*ch'ü*) poetic forms were all originally sung to musical accompaniment, but the *ci* in particular retains the character of a song poem. During the Tang, singing girls from Central Asia had popularized non-Chinese songs in the entertainment districts of Chinese cities. The *lu shi* and *jue ju* were sung to this new music, and the Chinese began to write new lyric to match. This evolved into the dominant form during the Song Dynasty.

There were a number of song patterns known throughout China. Chinese poets set a poem to an established song pattern, and specified which song pattern was to be used to accompany their *ci*. Approximately six hundred patterns exist, so there was great structural variation. Lines of unequal length ranged from one to over ten syllables, but rules fixed the number of syllables per line. Rhyme location varies. Popular origins are evident in the colloquial language of the *ci*. Song Dynasty poets wove the vigor and color of the tavern and markeplace into their poems. The *ci* was not melancholy, but it lent itself well to sentimental, lyrical composition. Early *ci* is also uncharacteristically concerned with romance, traditionally a minor theme in Chinese poetry.

The melodies underlying the *ci* poems have long been lost. In fact, they were sometimes lost well before the time of the Song Dynasty poet who wrote the *ci*. The poet then wrote the *ci* to match a newly composed melody or to match a standard literary pattern no longer associated with music. The *ci* was stretched by some poets to greater length than the *shi*. This verse form took its place alongside *lu shi, jue ju* and *shi* through the rest of Chinese history. It continues to be written. Mao Zedong (1893–1976) wrote poetry in the *ci* style.

The *Qu* (*ch'ü*) or Dramatic Verse of the Yuan Dynasty

The Yuan Dynasty (1271–1368) was China's great age of drama. Although the country was shattered by the Mongol invasion, great creative energies were unleashed. Chinese drama reached great heights, the novel found its beginnings, and fine poetry continued to be written. A new poetic genre emerged—the song or dramatic verse (*qu* 曲), written for drama. All the *shi* forms had been metrically regular. The *qu*, like the *ci*, has lines of irregular length, again reflecting their origins in song, but the *qu* diverges further than the *ci* from classical poetic norms. The Northern linguistic influence was changing syntax and vocabulary. The evolution of the Chinese language was also having an effect on poetry. Earlier rhyme schemes no longer worked. Tones were changing.

Qu are complex. Like the *ci*, poets wrote lyrics to established songs, although the songs came from a different repertory than the *ci*. One rhyme is maintained throughout the sequence of songs. One tonality is maintained throughout the musical system. *Qu* can vary in form and tune, but are patterned in a particular order. The complexity of the *qu* is offset somewhat by its use of colloquial spoken language. Its folk song origins are apparent, incorporating everyday speech, slang and common idioms. The Song Dynasty *ci* had been based on popular songs, but the range had broadened considerably with the *qu*. The *qu* was chanted or sung by cabaret girls, storytellers and actors. In the hands of the literati it was written as much to express exuberance over scenery, wine, love, friendship, humor and satire as somber political or social concerns.

There are two types of *qu*: the *san qu*, which were songs written independently and not intended for use in a drama, and *xi qu*, which were songs written for inclusion in a drama.

After the Yuan Dynasty no new poetic forms evolved. Poetry in every previous form continued to be written through the Ming (1368-1644) and Qing, but no new forms emerged. The mainstream of Chinese literary creativity had permanently shifted away from poetry to the play, the novel, and the short story.

Chinese Poetic Conventions

Readers should become familiar with the historical context in which Chinese poetry was written. There is a difference between civilized north China and the frontiers. Chinese culture emerged in the north and spread gradually toward the south. For example, in the Tang poetry, travel to or residence in the south is often the result of official banishment and forced relocation to an undesirable or even dangerous place. The south was provincial, malarial and semi-barbarian. Periodically throughout Chinese history, tribes from Central Asia invaded the north, pushing the Chinese off the northern plain into the south where, angry and homesick, they agitated to recover their lost homeland.

Conversely, the Chinese, when militarily strong, became expansionist and invaded the west, their armies carrying the Han and Tang empires across the Inner Asian steppes to the fringes of Europe. Trips to the south, recovery of the north, and military campaigns to the west should be understood in those contexts.

Poetic Imagery

Some Chinese poetic images will be unfamiliar to Western readers. Chinese poets describe the rivers as rising up to the clouds, or to the sky. Color distinctions are between blue, blue-green and green-black. Poets admire peach and apricot blossoms rather than cherry or apple blossoms. Jade is admired, not diamonds, and beautiful jade is white, not green. Exquisite flowers are peonies or chrysanthemums, not roses.

Colors, fragrance, ornaments, warm mists, plum blossoms, east wind, and personal items such as combs are frequently erotic. Paper folding fans, because of their shape, allude to the moon, and the moon is frequently a metaphor for deserted women. Autumn, not winter, is the season of melancholy and death. Dragons are benevolent creatures that live under water. Phoenixes do not rise from the ashes. Poets are mostly government bureaucrats.

A Poetic Education

Every educated Chinese was a poet. After the seventh century the aim of every Chinese male was to pass the Imperial exams leading to an official government career. For example, in the Tang dynasty because passing the government exams required poetic proficiency, all officials had to become poets.

Extensive study was required to pass the exams, which were tests of ascending difficulty. By the time the exam system reached its highest level of development during the Qing (Ch'ing) Dynasty, it was also necessary to pass the three school-entrance tests as a precondition to taking the civil service exams. The first was the district examination. Successful candidates went on to the prefectural exam, and if they passed they moved on the qualifying exam. Thereafter one began the tests required to enter the bureaucracy. There were three main exams: the provincial, the metropolitan and the palace examinations. Passing the provincial exam conferred upon the candidate the title of recommended man (ju ren 舉人). The real focus of the series of exams was the metropolitan exam, pass of which during the Tang Dynasty awarded the candidate the title of presented scholar (jin shi 進士) and entry into an official career.

During the Song Dynasty the palace exam was added, and the jin shi degree was conferred upon its successful candidates. This prestigious exam was conducted by the emperor, emphasized form, and was an indicator of how the candidate would fare in official life.

Most Chinese poets were scholar-officials who had gone through the education process and the ordeal of the exam. Some had to take the exam repeatedly to pass it. Others, like Chen Zi'ang, Du Fu, Meng Jiao 孟郊 (751–814), and Zhang Ji 張籍 (766–830), passed but did not have satisfactory public careers. Ironically, Meng Haoran 孟浩然 (689–740), prominent poet of the High Tang, never managed to pass the exam, and China's most celebrated poet Li Bai never even sat for the exam. But all were educated in the same body of literature and shared a common poetic tradition. The writing of poetry was a vocation and an avocation.

Introduction

Poetry remains a prominent feature of Chinese culture. Nowadays, educated Chinese do not have to write poetry, but they still read it and memorize it. An educated person can recite from memory poems from the standard poetic anthology *Three Hundred Tang Poems* 唐詩三百首 (*Tang Shi San Bai Shou*).

ROMANIZATION

This book uses Pinyin romanization. It is more congenial to speakers of Russian than English, and is not an improvement over any other romanization. But it was adopted by the Chinese government as the official system of romanization, so we are stuck with it. In any event, modern Mandarin Chinese, regardless of which system of romanization is chosen to represent it, little resembles the phonology of Chinese spoken a millennium ago. Those who are interested in the sound of "ancient" Chinese, as Tang-era Chinese is termed, may wish to read the extensive literature on the subject by Edward H. Schafer.

Some Pinyin symbols especially troublesome to English speakers are:

    c is pronounced *ts*

    q is pronounced *ch*

    x is pronounced *sh*

    z is pronounced *dz*

    zh is pronounced *j*

In addition:

    is shortened to an *ih* sound after c, ch, r, s, sh, z, and zh.

    u is pronounced ü after j, q, x and y.

The use of Pinyin to represent personal and place names which are already well known by another system of romanization may be confusing, e. g. *Chongqing* for *Chungking*. In such cases, the older forms (Wade-Giles Romanization system for Mandarin Chinese) appear in parentheses.

詩

The Poetry

詩

龜雖壽

老驥伏櫪，志在千里。
烈士暮年，壯心不已。

曹操
Cáo Cāo

∞

Cao Cao (Ts'ao Ts'ao) (A.D. 155–220) is one of the most famous generals in Chinese history, a warrior who figured prominently in events at the end of the Han Dynasty. Although merely the adopted grandson of a court eunuch 取 Cao Cao had imperial aspirations. The Han was overthrown by its own generals who, originally in service to the throne, became independent warlords and struggled for supremacy. In a three-way division of power, Cao Cao held the north against Liu Bei in the west and Sun Quan in the south. This was the origin of the Three Kingdoms period (A.D. 220-280). Cao Cao's attempts to become ruler failed. He died in 220 without having become emperor, but his son Cao Pi usurped the throne and named his state the Wei.

The tortoise lives a very long life. Even when it is old by our standards it still has many years of life remaining. This is a *si yan shi* 四言詩, an old style poem using the four-character line, and the only poem in this collection using this style. A major poetic evolution was underway when this poem was written: the change from the four-character line to the five-character line.

(See also poem No. 60 in this collection.)

Last Rays of the Setting Sun

龜	guī	tortoise
雖	suī	although
壽	shòu	longevity, old age
老	lǎo	old
驥	jì	a thoroughbred horse
伏	fú	prostrate, lie down
櫪	lì	a stable, manger
志	zhì	the will, determination
在	zài	at, in, on
千	qiān	one thousand
里	lǐ	mile (a Chinese mile, equivalent to one-third of a modern English mile)
烈	liè	burning, ardent, violent
士	shì	warrior
烈士		patriot, hero (Cao Cao is referring to himself)
暮	mù	sunset
年	nián	year
壯	zhuàng	strong, robust
心	xīn	heart
不	bú	no, not
已	yǐ	finish, come to an end

(See also poem No 60 in this collection.)

詩

蒿里行

白骨露于野，千里無雞鳴。
生民百遺一，念之斷人腸。

曹操
Cáo Cāo

∞

Cao Cao's (Ts'ao Ts'ao) cunning and cruelty are portrayed in endless plays, operas and movies. Unsurpassed at strategy and at reading his adversary's mind, Cao Cao used guile and treachery to defeat his enemies. Ironically, he was also a man of refinement and culture.

The Three kingdoms period is regarded as an exciting and romantic time. Cao Cao and the other major figures associated with it have become popular heroes. Every school child is familiar with their exploits. Here only the last section of the full 16-line poem is translated.

(See also poem No. 60 in this collection.)

蒿	hāo	wormwood, plants
里	lǐ	mile, village, residence
蒿里		a tomb
行	xíng	go
白	bái	white
骨	gǔ	bone
露	lù	expose, be exposed, disclose
于	yú	at, in
野	yě	field, wild area
千	qiān	thousand
里	lǐ	mile, village, residence
無	wú	not have
雞	jī	rooster
鳴	míng	to crow, sound made by a bird
生	shēng	to produce, be born, life, living
民	mín	person
生民		the common people
百	bǎi	hundred
遺	yí	to remain
一	yī	one, a, one remains out of a hundred

詩

念	niàn	think of, remember, recall
之	zhī	it
斷	duàn	cut, cut short
人	rén	person
腸	cháng	intestines, entrails
斷人腸		it cuts one's entrails (conventional phrase similar to our saying "it breaks one's heart")

(See also poem No 60 in this collection.)

七步詩

煮豆燃豆萁，豆在釜中泣。
本是同根生，相煎何太急。

曹植
Cáo Zhí

∞

Cao Zhi, son of general Cao Cao, was a talented poet and the first major poet to write in the five-character line form that had evolved during the Han.

Cao Zhi and his younger brother both suffered persecution at the hands of their older brother Cao Pi, who had become emperor and to whom this poem is addressed. Cao Pi held the power of life and death over Cao Zhi and demanded, on pain of death, that Cao Zhi compose a poem within the time required to step off seven paces. Cao Zhi succeeded. Owing to this, and the intervention of their mother, Cao Zhi was not executed.

Cao Zhi alludes to his brotherhood with Cao Pi, saying that they are beans in the same pot, grown from the same family root. Why is his brother in such a hurry to be rid of him?

詩

七	qī	seven
步	bù	a step, a pace
詩	shī	a poem
煮	zhǔ	to boil
豆	dòu	beans, soybeans
燃	rán	to burn
豆其		bean stalk (Chinese, to this day, burn bean stalks as fuel. After crops are harvested, residual materials such as stalks, vines and roots are used as fuel. Here the bean stalk is burning and roasting the beans)
豆	dòu	beans, soybeans
在	zài	at, in, on
釜	fǔ	cooking pot
中	zhōng	middle, in, within
泣	qì	to weep, shed tears, the beans begin to cry (for the rest of the poem, the beans address the burning bean stalks)
本	běn	originally, root, source, origin
是	shì	to be (here, we were)
同	tóng	the same
根	gēn	root, origin
生	shēng	to produce, be born, life, living

Continued ▶

相	xiāng	mutual, reciprocal, towards (here, towards us)
煎	jiān	to fry
何	hé	what, what reason, what for, why
太	tài	great, extreme
急	jí	haste, harsh

詩

敕勒歌

敕勒川，陰山下。
天似穹廬，籠蓋四野。
天蒼蒼，野茫茫。
風吹草低見牛羊。

無名氏
Anonymous

The vast northern prairies of China hold a fascination for the Chinese. This anonymous poem dating from the Northern and Southern Dynasties (A.D. 420-581) captures that feeling. It is a very popular poem. It was also the first free-verse poem (*ziyou shi* 自由詩) in Chinese. Remember the poem, because there is very little free-verse written in Chinese.

敕	chì	imperial order (here used only for sound)
勒	lè	to rein in a horse (here used only for sound)
敕勒		the name of an ethnic nationality, the ancestors of the Mongols (during the Northern and Southern Dynasties [A.D. 420-581] they lived in the northern part of modern Qinghai Province)
歌	gē	song
川	chuān	river (here it means a river plain)
敕勒川		place name (in northern Inner Mongolia)
陰	yīn	cloudy
山	shān	mountain
陰山		place name (in northern Inner Mongolia)
下	xià	beneath, under, to descend (*chi le chuan* 敕勒川), is located below
天	tiān	sky, heaven
似	sì	resemble
穹	qióng	arched
廬	lú	hut, house, cottage
穹廬		a yurt (Mongol felt tent with rounded top)

詩

籠	lǒng	cover, contain, literally a cage
蓋	gài	to cover
籠蓋		to cover
四	sì	four
野	yě	wild, wilderness, the wilds
四野		the four cardinal directions
天	tiān	sky, heaven
蒼	cāng	dark green (it can also be translated grey or blue (in poetry colors sometimes imply vast expanses of color, thus it may also be translated vast)
野	yě	wild, wilderness, the wilds
茫茫	máng	boundless
風	fēng	wind
吹	chuī	to blow
草	cǎo	grass
低	dī	low (here bent over low, because the grass is being blown by the prairie wind)
見	jiàn	to perceive, to appear
牛	niú	cow, ox
羊	yáng	sheep

登幽州台歌

前不見古人，
后不見來者；
念天地之悠悠，
獨愴然而涕下。

陳子昂
Chén Zǐ'áng

Chen Zi'ang was a low-ranking official of the early Tang Dynasty famous for both his poetry and his prose. He is regarded as the first major poet of the Tang. Chen reacted against the exaggerated style of court poetry popular during the Six Dynasties period and early Tang. His oppositional poetry, termed the *fu gu* 復古 (return to the ancient) style, stressed lean, formal verse and conservative Confucian morality. Many contemporary poets revered and emulated his style.

This poem is a song, therefore the lines are of uneven length. In this context *gu ren* 古人 and *lai zhe* 來者 both refer to heroes. The Tang expanded westward and needed stalwart soldiers to build its empire.

詩

登	dēng	climb
幽	yōu	remote, secluded, mysterious
州	zhōu	an administrative geographical region
幽州		place name (old name for Beijing)
台	tái	terrace (platform, if the reference is to the Great Wall it means a beacon tower (*fēng huǒ tái* 烽火台))
歌	gē	song
前	qián	before, formerly
不	bú	no, not
見	jiàn	see
古	gǔ	ancient
人	rén	person
後	hòu	after, hereafter, in the future
不	bú	no, not
見	jiàn	see
來	lái	come
者	zhě	one who…
念	niàn	think of, recall
天	tiān	heaven, sky
地	dì	earth
之	zhī	of, go, personal pronoun
悠	yōu	long, prolonged, drawn out

Continued ▶

獨	dú	alone
愴	chuàng	sad, sorrowful, disheartened
然	rán	an adverbial suffix, -ly, so
而	ér	consequently
涕	tì	a tear, to weep
下	xià	beneath, under, to descend

詩

詠柳

碧玉妝成一樹高，
萬條垂下綠絲絛。
不知細葉誰裁出？
二月春風似剪刀。

賀知章
Hè Zhīzhāng

∞

He Zhizhang was one of a group of poets from the southeast, and a renowned eccentric. He is also known for being Li Bai's mentor, the statesman-poet who introduced the young Li to the great Emperor Ming of Tang (685-762). He Zhizhang and Li Bai were bon vivants, two of the Eight Immortals of the Wine Cup, famous drinkers and carousers. Among the stories told about He Zhizhang is that while drunk he fell off his horse down a dry well where he came to rest snoring. Called the Madman of Siming, he led a life of jovial dissipation but nevertheless wrote very high quality poetry. The following poem is certainly regarded as an example of superior poetry. He asks if you know who cut the tree's delicate leaves. Of course, more than the tree's life is implied.

詠	yǒng	sing, chant, sing of
柳	liǔ	willow tree
碧	bì	green, the color of jade
玉	yù	jade
妝	zhuāng	to make up by use of cosmetics
成	chéng	complete
一	yí	a, one
樹	shù	tree (here used as a measure word: one tree's worth of height)
高	gāo	tall, high
萬	wàn	ten thousand
條	tiáo	measure word for long, thin things
垂	chuí	to droop, hang down
下	xià	down, below, under
綠	lǜ	green
絲	sī	silk
條	tāo	braid, braided silk ribbon

詩

不	bù	no, not
知	zhī	know
細	xì	delicate, fine, thin
葉	yè	leaf
誰	shuí	who
裁	cái	cut
出	chū	go out, come out (here a verb complement)
裁出		to cut off
二	èr	two, the second
月	yuè	moon, month
春	chūn	spring
風	fēng	wind
似	sì	resemble
剪	jiǎn	sciessors, clippers
刀	dāo	knife
剪刀		scissors

登鸛鵲樓

白日依山盡，黃河入海流。
欲窮千里目，更上一層樓。

王之渙
Wáng Zhīhuàn

∞

Wang Zhihuan was from Taiyuan, Shanxi Province, and traced his family origins to Shanxi and Xinjiang. Wang held an office of no particular importance and resigned the office in indignation. Thereafter he traveled over rivers and mountains both north and south of the Yellow River. Gao Shi became a good friend to Wang and wrote a poem to him. Wang Changling and Cui Guofu were also good friends of Wang's, and the group wrote much poetry together. Toward the end of his life Wang Zhihuan held a low county office in Hebei. He was known for his good character. He never harmed anyone, nor was he corrupt.

The Crane Magpie Tower was located in Shanxi Province.

詩

登	dēng	climb, ascend
鸛	guàn	crane
鵲	què	magpie
樓	lóu	multi-storied building
鸛鵲樓		a tower in Shanxi Province
白	bái	white
日	rì	sun
依	yī	lean against, descend, set
山	shān	mountain
盡	jìn	to exhaust, to finish
黃	huáng	yellow
河	hé	river
黃河		place name (the Yellow River)
入	rù	enter
海	hǎi	sea, ocean
流	liú	flow

Continued ▶

欲	yù	want
窮	qióng	exhausted, impoverished, used to the utmost (here it means to use one's eyes to the utmost, in other words, to see as far as one can)
千	qiān	thousand, many
里	lǐ	mile (a Chinese mile is equivalent to one-third of a modern English mile)
目	mù	eye, to eye, to look at, a sight, a vision
更	gèng	more, still more
上	shàng	above, on, to ascend
一	yì	one
層	céng	a story in a multi-storied building
樓	lóu	multi-storied building

詩

涼州詞

黃河遠上白云間，
一片孤城萬仞山。
羌笛何須怨楊柳，
春風不度玉門關。

王之渙
Wáng Zhīhuàn

∞

Wang Zhihuan comes across as an engaging person, impetuous, guileless and open. He is remembered merrily tapping rythm on his sword blade while chanting his poetry. There is a story that his drinking companions, the famous poets Gao Shi and Wang Changling, used to play a trick on him. They would secretly meet with visiting composers and singers and get them to feign uninterest in using Wang Zhihuan's poems in their songs.

Nevertheless, composers did base their popular songs on his poetry. Wang Zhihuan wrote very readable poems, intelligible even to the common people. He also wrote a large number of poems, but unfortunately only six survive in the *Tang Dynasty Poetry Collection* 全唐詩. They are considered excellent. The two in this book are his most famous. His poetry is widely known and often quoted.

Last Rays of the Setting Sun

涼	liáng	cool
州	zhōu	an administrative geographical region
涼州		place name (in modern Gansu Province)
詞	cí	a poem in the *ci* (*tz'u*) style
黃	huáng	yellow
河	hé	river
黃河		place name (The Yellow River)
遠	yuǎn	far, distant
上	shàng	over, above, ascend
白	bái	white
云	yún	clouds
間	jiān	between, among
一	yí	a, one
片	piàn	a piece, slice (in describing land it might be translated a stretch, a tract, a parcel, etc. Here it is a measure word for city (*chéng* 城), and need not be translated)
孤	gū	alone
城	chéng	city
一片孤城		a city alone
萬	wàn	ten thousand
仞	rèn	measure word meaning eight feet
山	shān	mountain

羌	qiāng	proper name (the Qiang tribe of western China)
笛	dí	bamboo flute
何	hé	what, why
須	xū	to need
怨	yuàn	find fault with, feel sad about
楊	yáng	poplar tree
柳	liǔ	willow tree
楊柳		the title of a song (its correct name was *Zhé Yáng Liǔ* 折楊柳, "Picking Poplars and Willow". It was sung when parting)
春	chūn	spring
風	fēng	wind
不	bú	no, not
度	dù	to pass, cross over
玉	yù	jade
門	mén	gate, door
關	guān	gate, a pass
玉門關		place name (in modern Gansu Province)

過故人莊

故人具雞黍，邀我至田家。
綠樹村邊合，青山郭外斜。
開軒面場圃，把酒話桑麻。
待到重陽日，還來就菊花。

孟浩然
Mèng Hàorán

Meng Haoran was the most prominent of the High Tang poets, a philosophic poet highly regarded by his contemporaries. He waited until he was in his forties before taking the imperial exams and, unfortunately, did not pass. Dissapointment over this failure led him to return to his mountain home in Hubei and live out his life as a recluse.

Here Meng awaits the Double-Ninth Festival, and will return to be close to the chrysanthemum. Chrysanthemum represent elegance, and it is his friend he is referring to. They also represent dignity and modesty, and are compared to gentlemen. The ninth month is the chrysanthemum month. Chrysanthemum are very popular in China. There is an annual Chrysanthemum Festival in modern Luoyang (Lo-yang).

詩

過	guò	to pass
故	gù	old
人	rén	person
故人		an old friend
莊	zhuāng	village
故	gù	old
人	rén	person
故人		an old friend
具	jù	prepare
雞	jī	chicken
黍	shǔ	millet (millet is a feed grain not a food grain, and is normally used for chicken feed. No one who can afford buy better grain would eat it)
雞黍		a simple meal
邀	yāo	to invite
我	wǒ	I, me
至	zhì	arrive
田	tián	field (as an adjective it would mean rustic, country)
家	jiā	home, family, establishment
田家		peasant house

Continued ▶

Last Rays of the Setting Sun

綠	lǜ	green
樹	shù	tree
村	cūn	village
邊	biān	side, beside
合	hé	go together, merge, to close (here to be surrounded by)
青	qīng	green
山	shān	mountain
郭	guō	city wall, the outer city wall (inner city walls are called *chéng* 城)
外	wài	outside (here, outside the city)
斜	xiá	slanting, tilted (here, the mountains slant)
開	kāi	to open
軒	xuān	house, door of house
面	miàn	surface, face, to face
場	chǎng	ground, ground on which rice is spread to dry
圃	pǔ	vegetable garden
把	bǎ	to take, to grasp
酒	jiǔ	wine
話	huà	speech, to speak
桑	sāng	mulberry
麻	má	hemp

詩

待	dài	wait (waiting for the arrival of the Double Ninth Festival)
到	dào	arrive
重	chóng	again
陽	yáng	sun
日	rì	day, sun
重陽日		Double Ninth Festival (during which one climbs a mountain and puts blossoms in one's hair)
還	huán	return
來	lái	come
就	jiù	then, be near to, approach, go, come enjoy the chrysanthemums with me
菊	jú	chrysanthemum
花	huā	flower, blossom
菊花		chrysanthemum

宿建德江

移舟泊煙渚，日暮客愁新。
野曠天低樹，江清月近人。

孟浩然
Mèng Hàorán

∞

Following Meng Haoran's failure in the imperial exams, he made a long tour of the Yangtze region. The scenes he saw on that trip inspired many of his poems. Meng's nature poems encompass a wide aesthetic range, showing both a quietistic appreciation of nature and an awe at China's scenery.

Here the poet lives on the Jiande River and moors at a misty islet.

詩

宿	sù	to reside, to spend the night	
建	jiàn	to establish	
德	dé	morality	
江	jiāng	river	
建德江		place name (the Jiande River)	
移	yí	to move across	
舟	zhōu	a boat	
泊	bó	to moor	
煙	yān	smoke, mist	
渚	zhǔ	islet	
日	rì	day, sun	
暮	mù	evening, sunset	
客	kè	guest	
愁	chóu	sad, melancholy	
新	xīn	new	
野	yě	wild, the wilds, a field	
曠	kuàng	vast, spacious	
天	tiān	heaven, sky	
低	dī	low	
樹	shù	tree (the sky comes down and meets the trees)	

Continued ▶

江	jiāng	river
清	qīng	clear
月	yuè	moon, month
近	jìn	near, close
人	rén	person (here the moon is close to me)

詩

春曉

春眠不覺曉，處處聞啼鳥。
夜來風雨聲，花落知多少。

孟浩然
Mèng Hàorán

∞

Meng Haoran has written a poem of the genre *Xi Chun* 惜春, melancholy poetry lamenting the passage of spring. The blossom petals fall, meaning spring will soon end.

The Chinese are equally fond of *Bei Qiu* 悲秋 poems, lamenting the passing of summer and the arrival of autumn.

This is a popular poem for memorization.

春	chūn	spring
曉	xiǎo	daybreak, dawn
春	chūn	spring
眠	mián	to sleep
不	bù	no, not
覺	jué	feel, sense, be aware of
曉	xiǎo	daybreak, dawn
處	chù	a place
處處		everywhere, everyplace
聞	wén	hear
啼	tí	chirp, sound made by birds
鳥	niǎo	bird
夜	yè	night
來	lái	come
夜來		(here meaning all night)
風	fēng	wind
雨	yǔ	rain
聲	shēng	sound

詩

花	huā	flower, blossom
落	luò	fall
知	zhī	know
多	duō	many
少	shǎo	few
多少		how many, how much, so many, so much
知多少		know how many (here perhaps better translated don't know how many)

別董大

千里黃云白日曛，
北風吹雁雪紛紛。
莫愁前路無知己，
天下誰人不識君！

高適
Gāo Shì

∞

Rising from poverty in Shandong Province, Gao Shi led an adventurous life. When young he fell in love with an actress, joined her theatrical company as a writer, and toured China with her. Later he went to Tibet as secretary to a high official. Eventually Gao became a soldier. Late in life he was made a marquis. Although he did not begin writing poetry until he was over fifty, he achieved fame as a poet. Gao Shi is known for poetry with a martial theme.

Here he bids farewell to a friend, and advises him not to worry about not having friends on the road ahead. Everyone knows who he is.

詩

別	bié	to separate, to part with, say goodbye to
董	dǒng	to direct, a director, surname
大	dà	great, large (here a person's given name)
董大		(Mr.) Dong Da (the oldest child of the Dong family)
千	qiān	thousand
里	lǐ	mile (a Chinese mile is equivalent to one-third of a modern English mile)
黃	huáng	yellow
雲	yún	cloud
白	bái	white
日	rì	sun, day
曛	xūn	sunset (here it should be translated as a color in order to retain parallelism with the third character *huáng* 黃)
北	běi	north
風	fēng	wind
吹	chuī	blow
雁	yàn	goose
雪	xuě	snow
紛紛	fēn	numerous, one after another, in great numbers

Continued ▶

莫	mò	do not
愁	chóu	to grieve, be anxious
前	qián	before, in front of
路	lù	road
無	wú	not, not have
知	zhī	know
己	jǐ	self
知己		intimate friends
天	tiān	heaven, sky
下	xià	beneath, under, to descend
天下		all under the sky, i.e. the world
誰	shuí	who
人	rén	person
不	bù	no, not
識	shí	recognize
君	jūn	you

雜詩

君自故鄉來，應知故鄉事。
來日綺窗前，寒梅著花未？

王維
Wáng Wéi

∞

Wang Wei (701-761) is one of China's great poets and a major poet during the peak of the Tang Dynasty. Born in Shanxi into a family of officials and literati, he left home for the capital at age sixteen with his younger brother. The Wang brothers achieved instant social success owing to their extraordinary literary talents. Wang Wei earned his *jinshi* degree at age twenty-three and was appointed Assistant Secretary for Music. Owing to a minor infraction he lost the position and was transfered to Shandong. Tiring of life in the provinces, Wang returned to the capital, suffered the loss of his wife, and again took office in 734. He was sent on a mission to the north-west frontier for several years and returned to continue a moderately successful career.

Here Wang Wei asks the stranger, on the day when he left, whether the scenery was beautiful outside the window in his hometown.

雜	zá	varied, mixed, miscellaneous
詩	shī	poem, poetry
君	jūn	gentleman ("you, sir...")
自	zì	from
故	gù	old
鄉	xiāng	town
故鄉		hometown
來	lái	come
應	yīng	should, ought to
知	zhī	know
故	gù	old
鄉	xiāng	town
故鄉		hometown
事	shì	matters, affairs, events
來	lái	come
日	rì	day
來日		the day when you come
綺	qǐ	beautiful, gorgeous (the literal meaning is a woven, figured silk damask)
窗	chuāng	window
前	qián	before, formerly

詩

寒	hán	cold
梅	méi	plum
著	zhuó	to bear
花	huā	flower, blossom
未	wèi	not yet

鹿柴

空山不見人，但聞人語響。
返景入深林，復照青苔上。

王維
Wáng Wéi

∞

Wang Wei bought a country estate about thirty miles south of Chang'an in the Zhongnan Mountains. He lived there intermittently and the contemplative, tranquil country life he led there figures prominently in his poetry.

Wang Wei enjoyed solitude, and periodically withdrew to lead the life of a recluse. He was a devout Buddhist and spent years quietly studying the scriptures.

詩

鹿	lù	deer
柴	zhài	firewood, brushwood (usually pronounced chái)
鹿柴		place name (Lu Zhai in modern Shaanxi Province)
空	kōng	empty
山	shān	mountain
不	bú	no, not
見	jiàn	see, perceive, appear
人	rén	person
但	dàn	only
聞	wén	to hear
人	rén	person
語	yǔ	talk
響	xiǎng	sound, noise
返	fǎn	return
景	jǐng	scenery, sunshine
返景		last rays of the setting sun
入	rù	enter
深	shēn	deep
林	lín	forest

Continued ▶

復	fù	again, to go back, to retrace
照	zhào	shine
青	qīng	dark green
苔	tái	moss
上	shàng	above, on, to ascend

詩

送元二使安西

渭城朝雨浥輕塵，
客舍青青柳色新。
勸君更盡一杯酒，
西出陽關無故人。

王維
Wáng Wéi

The poet urges his friend Yuan Er to have another cup of wine, because when Yuan Er goes to the far west he won't have any old fiiends there. This poem inspired a song which is usually played on the erhu violin or the Chinese zither. The song, which may date back to the Tang Dynasty, is still popular today. This poem also inspired an item in Ezra Pound's *Cathay*.

送	sòng	to send off
元	yuán	first, primary, unit, surname
二	èr	two, second
元二		(Mr.) Yuan Er (this would be a man's family nickname (*paihang* 排行) which shows his seniority among his siblings. It is used by a man's family or close friends. His name means Yuan-the-Second, the second child of the Yuan family. The oldest offspring would be named Yuan Da)
使	shǐ	to serve as an envoy
安	ān	tranquil
西	xī	west
安西		place name (in modern Xinjiang province)
渭	wèi	proper name (the Wei River, Shaanxi Province)
城	chéng	city
渭城		place name (in modern Shaanxi Province)
朝	zhāo	dawn, early morning
雨	yǔ	rain
浥	yì	to be wet
輕	qīng	light in weight
塵	chén	dust

詩

客	kè	guest	
舍	shè	cottage, shed, cabin	
青	qīng	green	
青			
柳	liǔ	willow tree	
色	sè	color	
新	xīn	new, fresh	
勸	quàn	persuade	
君	jūn	gentleman, "you, sir…	
更	gèng	more, even more	
盡	jìn	utmost, to the utmost, entirely (here to drink up)	
一	yì	a, one	
杯	bēi	cup, winecup	
酒	jiǔ	wine	
西	xī	west, westward	
出	chū	go out, come out	
陽	yáng	sun	
關	guān	a pass, mountain pass	
陽關		place name (Dunhuang in modern Gansu Province)	
無	wú	not, not have	
故	gù	old	
人	rén	person	
故人		old friend	

山居秋暝

空山新雨後，天氣晚來秋。
明月松間照，清泉石上流。
竹喧歸浣女，蓮動下漁舟。
隨意春芳歇，王孫自可留。

王維
Wáng Wéi

Wang Wei excelled at five-character lines and wrote much nature poetry. Partly because of his devotion to Buddhism, he withdrew from society for periods of seclusion. While in government service at Chang'an he would live in the Zhongnan Mountains, and during a period of exile lived on Mount Song near Luoyang (Lo-yang).

詩

山	shān	mountain
居	jū	reside, residence, cabin, cottage, hut
秋	qiū	autumn
暝	míng	dusk, sunset
空	kōng	empty
山	shān	mountain
新	xīn	new
雨	yǔ	rain
後	hòu	after
天	tiān	sky, heaven
氣	qì	air
天氣		weather
晚	wǎn	evening
來	lái	come
秋	qiū	autumn (here autumn weather)
明	míng	bright
月	yuè	moon
松	sōng	pine tree
間	jiān	among, between
照	zhào	shine

Continued ▶

清	qīng	clear
泉	quán	a spring, a fountain
石	shí	rock, stone
上	shàng	above, on, to ascend
流	liú	flow
竹	zhú	bamboo
喧	xuān	a noise (here the noice of the bamboo rattling in the wind)
歸	guī	return
浣	huàn	wash
女	nǚ	woman
浣女		a washerwoman
蓮	lián	lotus
動	dòng	move
下	xià	beneath, under, to descend (here to go down river)
漁	yú	fish
舟	zhōu	boat
漁舟		fishing boat

詩

隨	suí	follow, to accord with
意	yì	thought, meaning, desire
隨意		in accordanace with one's desires (here, the poet doesn't care whether the spring flowers wither or not)
春	chūn	spring
芳	fāng	fragrance
歇	xiē	finish, disappear
王	wáng	king, royal
孫	sūn	grandchild
王孫		(here Wang Wei refers to himself)
自	zì	self
可	kě	can, to be able
留	liú	to stay, leave behind

九月九日憶山東兄弟

獨在異鄉爲異客，
每逢佳節倍思親。
遙知兄弟登高處，
遍插茱萸少一人。

王維
Wáng Wéi

The ninth day of the ninth month is *Chongyang Jie* 重陽節, the Double Ninth Festival during which friends adorn their hair with sprigs of dogwood flowers, climb mountains together and drink toasts. The flowers are for protection from harm. The festival originated in the following folktale. A man met a fairy who warned him that on the ninth day of the ninth month death would come to the village. He should save himself by climbing to a high place out of danger. The man got the villagers and together they climbed a mountain. Afterwards when they came back down the mountain they found that all the animals in the village were dead.

詩

九	jiǔ	nine
月	yuè	moon, month
日	rì	sun, day
憶	yì	recall, recollect (here to miss)
山	shān	mountain
東	dōng	east
山東		place name (this Shangdong is in today's Shanxi Province, referring to the poet's hometown that is located in the eastern area of Mount Hua. It does not refer to today's Shangdong province, which is located in the eastern coastal area of China)
兄	xiōng	elder brother
弟	dì	younger brother
兄弟		brothers
獨	dú	single, alone
在	zài	at, in, on
異	yì	strange
鄉	xiāng	town, home village
爲	wéi	to be
異	yì	strange
客	kè	guest (refers to the poet)

Continued ▶

每	měi	each, every, every time
逢	féng	meet, encounter
佳	jiā	good, pleasant
節	jié	holiday
倍	bèi	twofold, double (he misses them twice as much because of the holiday)
思	sī	think of, to miss
親	qīn	a family relation
遙	yáo	far
知	zhī	know
兄	xiōng	elder brother
弟	dì	younger brother
兄弟		brothers
登	dēng	climb
高	gāo	high, tall
處	chù	place
遍	biàn	all
插	chā	to insert
茱萸	zhūyú	dogwood
少	shǎo	few, less
一	yì	a, one
人	rén	person (the "one less person" that is missing from the family outing is the poet himself)

詩

竹里館

獨坐幽篁里，彈琴復長嘯。
深林人不知，明月來相照。

王維
Wáng Wéi

∞

Wang Wei was not only a great poet, he was also a great landscape painter. The Song Dynasty poet Su Shi (1037–1101) remarked that in Wang Wei's poetry there is painting, and in his painting there is poetry. Landscape painting and Buddhism were major influences on Wang Wei's poetry.

竹	zhú	bamboo
里	lǐ	in, within, inside
館	guǎn	an inn, guest house, tavern (in this case it is more likely a small cottage constructed in a scenic glade by a bamboo grove or forest)
獨	dú	alone
坐	zuò	sit
幽	yōu	dark, secret, secluded
篁	huáng	bamboo grove
里	lǐ	in, within, inside
彈	tán	to play a musical instrument
琴	qín	Chinese 7-string zither
復	fù	again
長	cháng	long
嘯	xiào	to hum, to whistle
深	shēn	deep
林	lín	forest
人	rén	person
不	bù	no, not
知	zhī	know, nobody knows I'm here

詩

明	míng	bright
月	yuè	moon, month
來	lái	come
相	xiāng	reciprocal, each other, toward me
照	zhào	shine, shines on me

送別

山中相送罷，日暮掩柴扉。
春草明年綠，王孫歸不歸？

王維
Wáng Wéi

∞

When the An Lushan Rebellion broke out in 755, Wang Wei was unable to flee with the government and was captured by the rebels. To avoid serving the rebel regime he feigned illness, pretended to be deaf and dumb, and is said to have attempted suicide. Eventually he accepted a position in the rebel government. When the imperial government took back the capital, Wang Wei narrowly escaped being executed for collaboration. Sad poetry he had written lamenting the fate of the nation and the court was cited as proof of his loyalty to the throne. Wang resumed his official career, and was promoted to a position in the Council of State several years before his death.

Wang Wei sends off his friends. The grass will be green again next year, but will his friends return?

詩

送	sòng	send, send off	
別	bié	to separate, to part	
送別		to see someone off, a farewell visit	
山	shān	mountains	
中	zhōng	middle, in, within	
相	xiāng	reciprocal, each other, to me	
送	sòng	send, send off	
罷	bà	finish, after	
日	rì	sun, day	
暮	mù	to set	
掩	yǎn	to cover, to close	
柴	chái	sticks, firewood, brush	
扉	fēi	gate	
柴扉		a simple door for a hermit, made of firewood	
春	chūn	spring	
草	cǎo	grass	
明	míng	bright	
年	nián	year	
明年		next year	
綠	lǜ	green	

Continued ▶

王	wáng	king, royal
孫	sūn	grandchild
王孫		(here the poet's friends, a polite phrase)
歸	guī	to return
不	bù	no, not
歸	guī	to return

詩

早發白帝城

朝辭白帝彩雲間，
千里江陵一日還。
兩岸猿聲啼不住，
輕舟已過萬重山。

李白
Lǐ Bái

∞

Li Bai is the most famous of all Chinese poets, and his poetry is thought to represent Tang poetry at its highest level of development. He and Du Fu dominate Chinese poetry, and each is claimed to be the superior poet. The Chinese call Li Bai the Immortal of Poetry (*shi xian* 詩仙) and Du Fu the Saint of Poetry (*shi sheng* 詩聖).

Li was born in 701, perhaps in Central Asia, to a scholarly family and grew up in Sichuan Province about a hundred miles northeast of Chengdu. Li left his family at nineteen and began a roisterous, vagabond life that would take him all over the country and eventually to the court of the Emperor.

Baidi City (*Bai Di Cheng* 白帝城) is among colored clouds. A thousand miles lie between Baidi City and Jiang Ling.

Li's name appears in most Western sources as Li Po, which reflects an earlier pronunciation in Wade-Giles Romanization.

早	zǎo	early
發	fā	to issue, send forth, depart
白	bái	white
帝	dì	emperor
城	chéng	city
白帝城		place name (city in Sichuan Province)
朝	zhāo	early morning, dawn
辭	cí	bid farewell
白	bái	white
帝	dì	emperor
彩	cǎi	color, colored
雲	yún	cloud
間	jiān	among, in between
千	qiān	thousand
里	lǐ	mile (a Chinese mile is equivalent to one-third of a modern English mile)
江	jiāng	river
陵	líng	hill, mound, tomb
江陵		place name (Jiangling in Hubei Province)
一	yí	a, one
日	rì	sun, day
還	huán	return (here to arrive, he'll arrive in one day)

詩

兩	liǎng	two
岸	àn	shore, bank
猿	yuán	ape
聲	shēng	sound
啼	tí	cry of animals
不	bú	no, not
住	zhù	stop, dwell
輕	qīng	light in weight
舟	zhōu	boat
已	yǐ	already
過	guò	to pass
萬	wàn	ten thousand
重	chóng	to repeat, a layer
山	shān	mountain

望廬山瀑布

日照香爐生紫煙，
遙看瀑布掛前川。
飛流直下三千尺，
疑是銀河落九天。

李白
Lǐ Bái

∞

Li left home at nineteen to make his way in the world. He first lived with an eccentric religious hermit. Later as a swashbuckling knight-errant he wandered about the country righting wrongs for the oppressed and, according to a contemporary, dispatched a number of adversaries with his sword. Li traveled for years throughout north and central China, becoming one of China's most widely-travelled poets. He had begun the bohemian style that was to characterize his life. His poetry took years to mature. It wasn't until he was forty years old that he finally reached Chang'an and was received by the emperor.

A Chinese proverb says that good things come in three (*hao shi cheng san* 好事成三). Three and nine are also lucky numbers.

詩

望	wàng	look at from afar, to see in the distance
廬	lú	hut, cottage
山	shān	mountain
廬山		place name (Mt. Lu in Jiangxi Province)
瀑	pù	waterfall
布	bù	cloth
瀑布		waterfall
日	rì	sun, day
照	zhào	shine
香	xiāng	fragrance
爐	lú	a stove, a burner
香爐		place name (Xiang Lu is a mountain peak in the Lushan Range, Jiangxi Province)
生	shēng	to produce, be born, life, living
紫	zǐ	purple
煙	yān	smoke

Continued ▶

遙	yáo	distant, in the distance
看	kàn	look
瀑	pù	waterfall
布	bù	cloth
瀑布		waterfall
掛	guà	hang
前	qián	before, in front of
川	chuān	river
飛	fēi	to fly, flying
流	liú	flow
直	zhí	direct, straight
下	xià	beneath, under, to descend
三	sān	three
千	qiān	thousand
尺	chǐ	measure word meaning a foot (it's a traditional Chinese unit of length, which is still used today. In pre-modern China, the exact measurement of chi varied over time. In the Tang dynasty, 1 chi equals approximately .25 meters, which is around nine-tenths of a foot)

詩

疑	yí	doubt
是	shì	to be
銀	yín	silver
河	hé	river
銀河		the Milky Way
落	luò	descend
九	jiǔ	nine
天	tiān	heaven
九天		the Ninth Heaven, the highest of Taoist heavens

贈汪倫

李白乘舟將欲行，
忽聞岸上踏歌聲。
桃花潭水深千尺，
不及汪倫送我情。

李白
Lǐ Bái

∞

Li Bai was not distinguished as a scholar. Almost alone among Chinese men of letters, he never took the imperial exams. There were famous Chinese poets who did not pass the exams but later obtained official positions by other means. Li Bai however, never had a real official career of the sort appropriate for a man of his social standing and talent. He nevertheless attained national fame from his poetry, was befriended by the great poets of his day including Du Fu, and was finally honored by the emperor.

Li Bai says that although the lake is a thousand feet deep, it is not as deep as Wang Lun's feeling in sending him off.

詩

贈	zèng	to give a present
汪	wāng	a pool, a surname
倫	lún	constant, regular, ethical principles (here a person's given name)
汪倫		Mr. Wang Lun
李	Lǐ	surname
白	bái	white (here a person's given name)
李白		the poet Li Bai (Li Po)
乘	chéng	take
舟	zhōu	boat
將	jiāng	nearly, about to, to take
欲	yù	to want (here be about to)
行	xíng	to go
忽	hū	suddenly
聞	wén	to hear
岸	àn	shore, coast, bank of a river
上	shàng	above, on, to ascend
踏	tà	to stamp the feet, to tread on
歌	gē	song
踏歌		the name of a song of farewell
聲	shēng	sound

Continued ▶

桃	táo	peach, peach tree
花	huā	flower, blossom
潭	tán	a deep pond or lake
水	shuǐ	water
深	shēn	deep
千	qiān	a thousand
尺	chǐ	measure word meaning a foot (it's a traditional Chinese unit of length, which is still used today. In pre-modern China, the exact measurement of chi varied over time. In the Tang dynasty, 1 chi equals approximately .25 meters, which is around nine-tenths of a foot)
不	bù	no, not
及	jí	to reach to, to extend to
送	sòng	to send, to send off
我	wǒ	I, me
情	qíng	feeling, affection

詩

送友人

青山橫北郭，白水繞東城。
此地一爲別，孤蓬萬里征。
浮雲游子意，落日故人情。
揮手自茲去，蕭蕭班馬鳴。

李白
Lǐ Bái

∞

Li Bai did not have a successful public career but not for political reasons. His poetry was immensely popular. Emperor Ming of Tang (685–762) patronized him and because of Li's literary distinction made him a scholar of the Han-lin Academy. According to the commonly accepted story, Li is patronized by the emperor, given a horse from the imperial stables, writes enormously popular poetry, makes numerous court appearances, is constantly drunk, offends people at court, is discredited and sent away.

Li Bai was a skilled writer of *Jue Ju* but here has writen a *lü shi*. Li tells his departing friend -- as soon as you leave this place you, like tumbleweed (*gu peng* 成), are blown ten thousand miles by the wind. The traveller feels like a floating cloud, and sunset feels like your old friend.

送友人	sòng	send, send off
	yǒu	friend
	rén	person
青山橫北郭	qīng	green
	shān	mountain
	héng	horizontal, crosswise, at right angles
	běi	north
	guō	the outer city wall (ancient Chinese cities were enclosed by two walls and were composed of an inner city 內城 and an outer city 外城. Citizens lived in the inner city. Soldiers lived in the extended outer city)
白水繞東城	bái	white
	shuǐ	water
	rào	surround, to wind around
	dōng	east
	chéng	city
東城		the eastern part of the city

詩

此	cǐ	this
地	dì	place
一	yì	a, one, once (used with 就 it means as soon as or no sooner than. This common grammatical structure, yi X jiu Y, means once X occurs then Y is the result. In this poem (*jiu* 就) should appear before the word (*gu* 孤) in the fourth line, but it is understood and has been omitted)
爲	wèi	to be
別	bié	separate, apart
孤	gū	alone
蓬	péng	tangles of wild underbrush, tumbleweed
孤蓬		tangles of wild underbrush, tumbleweeds, which are blown around by the wind (metaphor for a lone traveler)
萬	wàn	ten thousand
里	lǐ	mile (a Chinese mile is equivalent to one-third of a modern English mile)
征	zhēng	go, go on a journey or expedition
浮	fú	float, drift
雲	yún	cloud
游	yóu	to swim, float, drift, a travel
子	zǐ	noun suffix
游子		a traveller
意	yì	an idea, meaning, sentiment (here a feeling, the traveller feels like…)

Continued ▶

— 73 —

落	luò	descend
日	rì	sun, day
故	gù	old
故人		old friend
情	qíng	feeling
揮	huī	to wave
手	shǒu	hand
揮手		wave goodbye to an old friend
自	zì	from
茲	zī	this, this place, here (this character used alternately with *ci* 此)
自茲		from now on
去	qù	go
蕭蕭	xiāo	neighing of horses, sound made by an animal
班	bān	separate from, depart, withdraw from
馬	mǎ	horse
鳴	míng	sound made by an animal

詩

送孟浩然之廣陵

故人西辭黃鶴樓，
煙花三月下揚州 。
孤帆遠影碧空盡 ，
唯見長江天際流 。

李白
Lǐ Bái

∞

Li wrote poetry by invitation for the imperial court but, due to his intemperance, his court career was brief. Three years after his arrival in the capital Li set out for a tour of the country. By then he had become a famous figure throughout the empire. A national celebrity, scholars and poets vied for his companionship wherever he went. He had as his friends many of the famous poets of the day. Here Li bids farewell to the great Meng Haoran. There is a legend that Li inscribed this poem inside the Yellow Crane Tower 黃鶴樓.

送	sòng	to send (off)
孟	mèng	surname
浩	hào	proper name
然	rán	proper name
孟浩然		the famous poet Meng Haoran (whose poems appear in this collection, pgs. 44, 48, 51)
之	zhī	to go
廣	guǎng	broad
陵	líng	hill, mound, imperial tomb
廣陵		place name (modern Yang Zhou in Jiangsu Province)
故	gù	old
人	rén	person
故人		old friend
西	xī	west
辭	cí	depart, bid farewell
黃	huáng	yellow
鶴	hè	crane
樓	lóu	multi-storied building
黃鶴樓		Yellow Crane Pavillion in Hubei Province (it still exists)

詩

煙	yān	smoke, mist
花	huā	flower, blossom
三	sān	three, third
月	yuè	moon, month
下	xià	beneath, under, to descend (his friend is going down the Yangtze)
揚	yáng	raise, scatter, spread
州	zhōu	a geographical region
揚州		place name (in Jiangsu Province)
孤	gū	alone
帆	fān	to sail
遠	yuǎn	far, distant
影	yǐng	shadow
碧	bì	jade, the color jade green
空	kōng	empty, emptiness (here the sky)
盡	jìn	utmost, entirely, to use up (the sailboat moves farther and farther away until it is no longer visible)

Continued ▶

唯	wéi	only
見	jiàn	see
長	cháng	long
江	jiāng	river
長江		place name (the Yangtze River)
天	tiān	sky, heaven
際	jì	border, boundary
流	liú	to flow

詩

望天門山

天門中斷楚江開，
碧水東流至此回。
兩岸青山相對出，
孤帆一片日邊來。

李白
Lǐ Bái

∞

Li Bai was the great rebel of Chinese poetry. He rebelled against all conventions, insulted high officials and was even irreverent toward the emperor. Li abandonded himself to wine, the splendors of nature, revelry and romance. (he married three times). Li was a big man who recited poetry in a loud voice and had a gargantuan capacity for drink.

His composing was inspired. He did not compose with deliberation but dashed off poems in great proliferation, even when dead drunk. He does not, like many other poets, write satire or allegory. Li does not write of death. His works have an exuberance, thrilling in flowers, birds, colors, the dawn, the night, stars, young women. His is a voracious appetite for life. Called an Immortal of Poetry (*Shi Xian* 詩仙), Li Bai is also China's great romantic.

Here Li Bai looks out over the waters of the Yangtze.

望	wàng	look, peer, see in the distance
天	tiān	sky, heaven
門	mén	gate, door
山	shān	mountain
天門山		place name (Mount Tianmen in Anhui Province)
天	tiān	sky, heaven
門	mén	gate, door
中	zhōng	middle, in, within
斷	duàn	break off
中斷		to be cut in the middle (here the mountain is cut in the middle by the river, thus it is called a mén 門)
楚	chǔ	place name (Chu, feudal state 740-230 B.C. Modern Hubei)
江	jiāng	river
楚江		the Yangtze River
開	kāi	open (here the river goes through the mountain)
碧	bì	green, jade color
水	shuǐ	water
東	dōng	east, eastward
流	liú	to flow
至	zhì	reach, arrive
此	cǐ	this, here
回	huí	return (here the river flows around in a whirlpool)

詩

兩	liǎng	two
岸	àn	riverbank, shore, coast
青	qīng	green
山	shān	mountain
相	xiāng	reciprocal, each other
對	duì	to face
出	chū	come out, go out, emerge (here the mountains emerge)
孤	gū	alone, solitary
帆	fān	a sail
一	yí	a, one
片	piàn	a measure word for thin flat objects
日	rì	sun, day
邊	biān	side, beside, boundary, border, edge
來	lái	come

靜夜思

床前明月光，疑是地上霜。
舉頭望明月，低頭思故鄉。

李白
Lǐ Bái

∞

Li was traveling in the Yangtze during the An Lushan Rebellion and was not involved. Later however, he was implicated in the insurrection of the Prince of Yong, a son of the Brilliant Emperor. Li was imprisoned following the defeat of the Prince of Yong and exiled to the extreme southwest of China. He returned to central China following an amnesty and died of illness in 762. A legend evolved about Li Bai's death. He is said to have leaned out of a boat to embrace the reflection of the moon on the water, fallen into the lake and drowned.

Jing Ye Si is probably the most beloved poem in Chinese. If a Chinese knows only one poem by heart, it will be this poem.

詩

靜	jìng	silent
夜	yè	night
思	sī	a thought, to think, reflect
床	chuáng	bed
前	qián	before, in front of
明	míng	bright
月	yuè	moon
光	guāng	brilliant
疑	yí	unsure, uncertain, to suspect
是	shì	to be, is
地	dì	ground
上	shàng	above, on, to ascend
霜	shuāng	frost
舉	jǔ	to raise, to lift
頭	tóu	head
望	wàng	look at
明	míng	bright
月	yuè	moon

Continued ▶

低	dī	to lower
頭	tóu	head
思	sī	a thought, to think, reflect
故	gù	old
鄉	xiāng	home, hometown

桃花溪

隱隱飛橋隔野煙，
石磯西畔問漁船。
桃花盡日隨流水，
洞在青溪何處邊？

張旭
Zhāng Xù

∞

Zhang Xu was a gifted poet and, as one of the Eight Immortals of the Winecup, was a carousing companion of the poet Li Bai. Zhang was a drunkard and wildly eccentric. Called the Immortal of Calligraphy (*shu sheng* 詩詩), he was famous for his superb grass-style calligraphy which he could dash off even when completely drunk.

This poem alludes to the famous poem Peach Blossom Spring by Tao Yuanming 陶淵明 (A.D. 365-427). That poem, a Shangri-La myth, tells the story of a fisherman who follows a stream to its source in a peach tree grove, and discovers a utopian community. Cut off since the Qin Dynasty, the community lives in peace, unaware of the outside world. The fisherman lived there a while, returned home to tell his story, but then could never find his way back to the Peach Blossom Spring.

桃	táo	peach
花	huā	blossom
溪	xī	stream, river
隱隱	yǐn	hidden, secret, to conceal (here hidden from view, indistinct)
飛	fēi	to fly (here to span, the bridge which spans the river)
橋	qiáo	bridge
隔	gé	separate(d)
野	yě	wild, the wilds
煙	yān	smoke, haze, mist, wilds and mist lie between (separate) the poet and the bridge, so the bridge is seen only faintly
石	shí	rock, stone
磯	jī	breakwater, rocks extending into the water, a jetty
西	xī	west
畔	pàn	bank, shore
問	wèn	to ask (here the poet, who is on the west side of the jetty, asks…)
漁	yú	fish
船	chuán	boat
漁船		fishing boat (here people fishing from a boat, fishers)

詩

桃	táo	peach
花	huā	blossom
盡	jìn	to exhaust, to use up
日	rì	sun, day
盡日		all day long
隨	suí	to follow
流	liú	flow, flowing
水	shuǐ	water (the peach blossoms fall into the water all day and follow the current)
洞	dòng	a cave, grotto, hole
在	zài	at, in, on
青	qīng	green
溪	xī	stream, river
何	hé	what
處	chù	place
邊	biān	side, beside (the poet asks, "where along the banks of this stream is the grotto that leads to the Peach Blossom Spring?")

涼州詞

葡萄美酒夜光杯，
欲飲琵琶馬上催。
醉臥沙場君莫笑，
古來征戰几人回？

王翰
Wáng Hàn

∞

Wang Han was from Taiyuan in Shanxi. We don't know his birth or death dates but we do know that he had a turbulent career. As a brilliant young man, he was supported by the patronage of a powerful governor. Wang received an office and began a meteoric rise to high position--prime minister, secretary of war and even higher. But his patron fell from power and, lacking his patron's support, Wang tumbled down the ladder of success as quickly as he had risen. Sadly, Wang Han ended his days in a lowly army position, carousing with ruffians and ne'er-do-wells.

Here Wang Han writes in the persona of a general on a military expedition to western China. The images are those of the far West. The general pleads--don't laugh at him for sleeping drunk on the battlefield.

詩

涼	liáng	cold
州	zhōu	a geographical region
涼州		place name (in modern Gansu Province)
詞	cí	poem in the *ci* style, the lyric.
葡	pú	vine, grape
萄	táo	character used to translate sound of foreign word
葡萄		grape
美	měi	excellent, delicious
酒	jiǔ	wine
夜	yè	night
光	guāng	light
夜光		moonlight
杯	bēi	a glass
夜光杯		moonlight glass (a type of drinking glass made of jade. They are still produced in China)

Continued ▶

欲	yù	want
飲	yǐn	drink
琵	pí	character used to transliterate sound of foreign words
琶	pá	character used to transliterate sound of foreign words
琵琶		guitar used by barbarian tribes in western China
馬	mǎ	horse
上	shàng	above, on, to ascend
催	cuī	to urge (the sound of the pipa urges him to mount his horse)
醉	zuì	intoxicated
臥	wò	sleep
沙	shā	sand
場	chǎng	ground
沙場		sandy ground (here a battlefield. Tang Dynasty battles were fought in the deserts of the far West, in Central Asia)
君	jūn	you
莫	mò	don't
笑	xiào	laugh

詩

古來	gǔ	old, ancient
來	lái	come
古來		since olden times
征	zhēng	to reduce to submission, to conquer
戰	zhàn	battle, war
征戰		to fight a battle
幾	jǐ	how many, how much
人	rén	person
回	huí	return

江畔獨步尋花

黃四娘家花滿蹊，
千朵萬朵壓枝低。
留連戲蝶時時舞，
自在嬌鶯恰恰啼。

杜甫
Dù Fǔ

∞

Revered as China's greatest poet, Du Fu (Tu Fu) is the finest master of the art of poetry. He was born into a family of literary distinction. His grandfather was a prominent poet, his uncle a recognized Confucian scholar.

Du Fu failed the imperial exams three times. He was unable to find a patron in the capital, nor did he impress the court sufficiently with his literary compositions to get a position. Finally in 755 he obtained a minor post. Soon however, the An Lushan rebels siezed the capital and Du Fu fled to serve the imperial court in exile.

詩

江	jiāng	river
畔	pàn	shore, bank
獨	dú	alone
步	bù	a step, on foot
尋	xún	search for
花	huā	flower, blossom
黃	huáng	yellow (here it is the surname of the person)
四	sì	four
娘	niáng	mother (in the Tang dynasty it is a common used term to refer to a young woman)
黃四娘		a person's name
家	jiā	home, family, establishment
花	huā	flower, blossom
滿	mǎn	to fill, full
蹊	xī	footpath
千	qiān	one thousand, many
朵	duǒ	measure word for flower
萬	wàn	ten thousand
朵	duǒ	measure word for flower
壓	yā	to press, weigh on
枝	zhī	branch
低	dī	low

Continued ▶

留	liú	to keep, to detain, to entertain
連	lián	to connect, to join
留連		reluctant to leave, can't bear to part
戲	xì	to play with
蝶	dié	butterfly
時	shí	time
時時		incessantly
舞	wǔ	to dance
自	zì	self
在	zài	at, in, on
自在		at ease, comfortable, unrestrained
嬌	jiāo	lovely, charming
鶯	yīng	oriole
恰恰	qià	happily, fortunately
啼	tí	to chirp, sound made by a bird

詩

春望

國破山河在，城春草木深。
感時花濺淚，恨別鳥驚心。
烽火連三月，家書抵萬金。
白頭搔更短，渾欲不勝簪。

杜甫
Dù Fǔ

∞

The An Lushan Rebellion captured Chang'an and set the Tang emperor to flight. Du Fu wrote this poem during the rebellion as insurgent troops occupied the capital. Although Du Fu's position—supervisor of a weapons storehouse—was too low to be affected, he couldn't leave Chang'an.

For the foliage to have been thick in spring has an ominous meaning for the Chinese reader of this poem. In China, trees and shrubs are pruned back severely in the spring. If they are growing thickly it is because order has broken down. There is no one to take care of them.

Notice Du Fu's powers of description—how he personifies the scenery. He was so affected by the war that he felt empathy even for plants—the flowers shed tears.

春	chūn	spring
望	wàng	to gaze at, to look at from afar
國	guó	country, nation
破	pò	to break
山	shān	mountain
河	hé	river
在	zài	at, in, on
城	chéng	city
春	chūn	spring
草	cǎo	grass
木	mù	tree
深	shēn	deep (here luxurious)
感	gǎn	feel, to be touched by
時	shí	events, current events (*shi* means events of the time)
花	huā	flower
濺	jiàn	to splash (here water splashing from a plant when it is being watered, it is the verb of this sentence)
淚	lèi	tears

詩

恨	hèn	sorrow, to feel sorrow
別	bié	separate (Du Fu is separated from his family)
鳥	niǎo	bird
驚	jīng	frightened
心	xīn	heart (the poet hears the birds singing sorrowfully and thinks they also feel sorry for him. This parallels the sad current events touching the poet and the flowers shedding tears)
烽	fēng	a beacon
火	huǒ	fire (beacon fires set by sentries atop the wall to warn of the approach of the enemy. In other words, to be at war)
連	lián	all together, continuously
三	sān	three
月	yuè	moon, month
家	jiā	family
書	shū	write, writings (a letter from the poet's family)
抵	dǐ	worth
萬	wàn	ten thousand
金	jīn	gold pieces

Continued ▶

白	bái	white
頭	tóu	head (here it means hair)
搔	sāo	scratch (in China, scratching one's hair indicates sorrow or mental anguish rather than confusion)
更	gèng	more
短	duǎn	short
渾	hún	almost
欲	yù	want
不	bú	no, not
勝	shèng	able to (bear or hold up)
簪	zān	barrette, hair clasp (the poet is saying that his hair was already white and thin with age. Sorrowfully scratching his hair has made it even thinner, …so thin that a barrette won't hold his hair up)

詩

登高

風急天高猿嘯哀，
渚清沙白鳥飛回。
無邊落木蕭蕭下，
不盡長江滾滾來。

杜甫
Dù Fǔ

∞

Dùˇ Fu was given a post in the chancellery. Eventually his outspoken behavior got him demoted and exiled to Shanxi. In 759 Dù Fu resigned his post and traveled to Chengdu, Sichuan where he spent the final decade of his life. It was a productive period. Over half of his life's poetry was written in Chengdu.

In this poem you will find both alliteration and parallelism. The parallelism is particularly pronounced; *wu bian* 無邊 and *bu jin* 不盡, *xiao xiao* 蕭蕭 and *gun gun* 滾滾. Dù Fǔ is called the master of parallelism.

登	dēng	climb
高	gāo	high, tall
風	fēng	wind
急	jí	agitated, hurried, anxious
天	tiān	sky, heaven
高	gāo	high, tall
猿	yuán	ape
嘯	xiào	cry of an ape, scream, screech, etc.
哀	āi	sad
渚	zhǔ	islet
清	qīng	clear
沙	shā	sand
白	bái	white
鳥	niǎo	bird
飛	fēi	fly
回	huí	return, circle (the birds fly in a circle. Usually pronounced *huí*. Here the pronunciation should rhyme)

詩

無	wú	not have, isn't, aren't
邊	biān	side, beside, edge, frontier
無邊		endless, endlessly
落	luò	drop down
木	mù	wood, tree (here leaves, endlessly falling leaves)
蕭蕭	xiāo	a sighing, whispering sound
下	xià	under, beneath, to descend
不	bú	no, not
盡	jìn	exhaust, use up
不盡		inexhaustable, endless
長	cháng	long
江	jiāng	river
長江		the Yangtze River
滾滾	gǔn	to roll, billow, surge
來	lái	come

前出塞

挽弓當挽強，用箭當用長。
射人先射馬，擒賊先擒王。
殺人亦有限，列國自有疆。
苟能制侵陵，豈在多殺傷。

杜甫
Dù Fǔ

∞

Dù Fǔ composed with great technical skill. He wrote in the newer verse forms, executing the *lü shi* sonnet with great virtuosity.

Here Du Fǔ gives some advice on waging war. When you go to fight the enemy, first kill their horses. Don't kill any more people than necessary, and the number of enemies you kill isn't as important as capturing the enemy king. If the encroachment is stopped, it is then not meaningful to kill any more people in the war.

詩

前	qián	forward, former, earlier
出	chū	go out, come out
塞	sài	fill in, to stop up (here *sài* means one of the gates or passes through the great wall. A *chu sai shi* 出塞詩 is a poem about warfare, a general category of Chinese poetry. Dǔ Fu makes a distinction between his earlier war poetry (*Qian Chu Sai* 前出塞) and his later war poetry (*Hou Chu Sai* 後出塞))
挽	wǎn	to draw, as in to draw a bow and arrow
弓	gōng	bow
當	dāng	ought to
挽	wǎn	to draw, as in to draw a bow and arrow
強	qiáng	strong, forcefully
用	yòng	use
箭	jiàn	arrow
當	dāng	ought to
用	yòng	use
長	cháng	long (here long arrows)
射	shè	to shoot (here to kill)
人	rén	person
先	xiān	first, before, beforehand
射	shè	to shoot (here to kill)
馬	mǎ	horses

Continued ▶

擒	qín	capture
賊	zéi	enemy
先	xiān	first, before, beforehand
擒	qín	capture
王	wáng	king
殺	shā	kill
人	rén	person
亦	yì	also (same as the modern *yě* 也, you also ought to…)
有	yǒu	exist, have
限	xiàn	limits
列	liè	each, every
國	guó	country, nation
自	zì	self, itself
有	yǒu	exist, have
疆	jiāng	borders
苟	gǒu	if
能	néng	able, can
制	zhì	stop
侵	qīn	invade, attack
陵	líng	hill, mound, imperial tombs
侵陵		to invade the area

詩

豈	qǐ	how
在	zài	at, in, on
多	duō	more, numerous
殺	shā	kill
傷	shāng	wound

自京赴奉先縣
詠懷五百字

朱門酒肉臭，路有凍死骨。
榮枯咫尺異，惆悵難再述。

杜甫
Dù Fǔ

∞

Dù Fǔ believed in strict Confucian morality in government and attention to the welfare of the people. His poetry frequently portrays the suffering and unjust treatment of the common people. A sober realist, Dù Fǔ frequently addresses themes of sadness and death.

A red door indicates a wealthy house. On the street outside the red door, people freeze. Inside, the meat is so plentiful it goes rancid.

These four lines are the most famous lines of this long 500-character poem, or perhaps, the most famous lines from Dù Fǔ.

詩

自	zì	from
京	jīng	capital (here Chang'an)
赴	fù	to go to
奉	fèng	receive, offer, serve
先	xiān	first, front, before
縣	xiàn	county
奉先		place name (Feng Xian County)
詠	yǒng	sing, chant
懷	huái	cherish
詠懷		to chant
五	wǔ	five
百	bǎi	hundred
字	zì	Chinese character
五百字		five hundred Chinese characters (a poetic composition written by Dù Fǔ of five-word lines in the "old style". In total, it has approximately five hundred Chinese characters)
朱	zhū	red
門	mén	gate, door
酒	jiǔ	wine
肉	ròu	meat
臭	chòu	rotten, rancid

Continued ▶

路	lù	road, street, on the street outside the red door
有	yǒu	have, exist
凍	dòng	freeze
死	sǐ	death
骨	gǔ	bone
榮	róng	to flourish (here life of luxury)
枯	kū	to wither (here life of poverty)
咫	zhǐ	an ancient unit of length equal to 8 Chinese inches (*cùn* 寸)
尺	chǐ	measure word meaning a foot (it's a traditional Chinese unit of length, which is still used today. In pre-modern China, the exact measurement of chi varied over time. In the Tang dynasty, 1 chi equals approximately .25 meters, which is around nine-tenths of a foot)
咫尺		very close
異	yì	different
惆	chóu	disappointed
悵	chàng	disappointed, dissatisfied, depressed
惆悵		disconsolate, melancholy
難	nán	difficult
再	zài	again
述	shù	say, relate (this last line means "it is difficult for me to talk about this melancholy situation")

詩

絶句

兩個黃鸝鳴翠柳，
一行白鷺上青天。
窗含西嶺千秋雪，
門泊東吳萬里船。

杜甫
Dù Fǔ

∞

In A.D. 765 Dù Fu began a journey down the Yangtze. Unfortunately his health broke and he was forced to stop and convalesce for two years at Kuizhou. It is during his Kuizhou period that literary critics discern a turning point in his poetry--the appearance of multiple meanings, the beginning of poetic ambiguity. He resumed his trip in 768 but again fell ill and died near Lake Dongting in 770.

A thousand autumn snows fall on the mountain range. The boat is moored by the gate and Eastern Wu is 10,000 miles away. Note Dù Fu's parallelism and his visual sense--colors, birds.

絕	jué	to cut off, to break off
句	jù	a sentence, a line of poetry
絕句		a *jue ju* (chueh-chu), a quatrain
兩	liǎng	two
個	gè	classifier
黃	huáng	yellow
鸝	lí	oriole
黃鸝		oriole
鳴	míng	chirp (sound made by birds, animals)
翠	cuì	emerald green, blue green (kingfisher, hummingbird)
柳	liǔ	willow tree
一	yì	a, one
行	háng	line (here a line of birds flying)
白	bái	white
鷺	lù	the egret
白鷺		egret
上	shàng	above, on, to ascend
青	qīng	green, blue
天	tiān	sky

詩

窗	chuāng	window
含	hán	to contain, to hold
西	xī	west
嶺	lǐng	mountain range
千	qiān	thousand
秋	qiū	autumn
雪	xuě	snow
門	mén	gate, door
泊	bó	to moor, to anchor a boat
東	dōng	east
吳	wú	place name (it always refers to the lower Yangtze River region, which includes a large area of today's Jiangsu Province)
東吳		place name (it originally referred to the Eastern Wu (222-280) during the Three Kingdom period (220-280), which occupied a large part of today's Jiangsu Province in the lower reaches of the Yangtze River)
萬	wàn	ten thousand
里	lǐ	mile (a Chinese mile is equivalent to one-third of a modern English mile)
船	chuán	boat

— 111 —

逢雪宿芙蓉山主人

日暮蒼山遠，天寒白屋貧。
柴門聞犬吠，風雪夜歸人。

劉長卿
Liú Chángqīng

∞

Liu Changqing was a Tang Dynasty official whose poetry enjoyed considerable popularity among his contemporaries. His skill at composing five-character poems was particularly admired. Many of his poems depict simple pastoral or rustic scenes.

Here the poet has come back to his friend's house. This family is poor. The front gate is made of sticks (*chai men* 柴門). If the family were wealthy they would have a red gate (*zhu men* 朱門).

詩

逢	féng	to meet, happen
雪	xuě	snow
宿	sù	to lodge for the night
芙	fú	lotus
蓉	róng	lotus
芙蓉		lotus
山	shān	mountain
芙蓉山		place name (Mount Furong)
主	zhǔ	a master, owner
人	rén	person
主人		host
日	rì	sun, day
暮	mù	evening, sunset
蒼	cāng	dark green, blue, grey, dark
山	shān	mountain
遠	yuǎn	far, distant
天	tiān	sky, heaven
寒	hán	cold
白	bái	white
屋	wū	house, room
貧	pín	poor

Continued ▶

柴	chái	wood, firewood
門	mén	door, gate
聞	wén	to hear
犬	quǎn	dog
吠	fèi	to bark
風	fēng	wind
雪	xuě	snow
夜	yè	night
歸	guī	to return
人	rén	person

詩

滁州西澗

獨憐幽草澗邊生，
上有黃鸝深樹鳴。
春潮帶雨晚來急，
野渡無人舟自橫。

韋應物
Wěi Yìngwù

Wei Yingwu had an unusual life. He began his career as a bodyguard of the Brilliant Emperor but, following a period of study, gained appointment to civil posts. Wei rose to a number of important positions, including Governor of Suzhou. He was apolitical and was known for his excellent character.

At a secluded ferry slip a lone boat drifts in the water, and Wei Yingwu enjoys his solitude.

滁	chú	place name (the Chu River which joins the Yangtze River near Nanjing (Nan-ching))
州	zhōu	a region
滁州		place name (in Anhui Province near Nanjing)
西	xī	west
澗	jiàn	gully, ravine, a mountain torrent
獨	dú	alone, only
憐	lián	to like, to love
幽	yōu	secluded, secret
草	cǎo	grass
澗	jiàn	gully, ravine, a mountain torrent
邊	biān	side, beside
生	shēng	to produce, be born, life, living (here the grass growing beside the gully)
上	shàng	above, on, to ascend
有	yǒu	exist, to have
黃	huáng	yellow
鸝	lí	oriole
深	shēn	deep, deep in
樹	shù	tree
鳴	míng	the cry of a bird, animal

詩

春	chūn	spring
潮	cháo	tide, spring flood(s)
帶	dài	to carry
雨	yǔ	rain
晚	wǎn	evening
來	lái	to come
晚來		at dusk, close to evening
急	jí	urgent, anxious, hastily
野	yě	wild
渡	dù	to cross over, to ferry over a river, a ferry slip, a river crossing site
無	wú	no, not, haven't
人	rén	person
舟	zhōu	boat
自	zì	self
橫	héng	crosswise, horizontal, to be at right angles (here the boat is adrift, not moored, but left to float loose)

漁歌子

西塞山前白鷺飛，
桃花流水鱖魚肥。
青箬笠，綠蓑衣，
斜風細雨不須歸。

張志和
Zhāng Zhìhé

∞

Zhang Zhihe served as an official under the emperor Su of the Tang. He was banished from the capital but soon pardoned in a general amnesty. He did not return to an official career, however, but became a wandering recluse. Zhang lived on a boat and fished, but didn't use bait because he didn't care whether or not he caught fish. He turned down the offer of a home because he preferred to "follow the gulls into cloudland". He called himself the Old Fisherman of the Mist and Waters.

Zhang left few poems and only this poem is widely known. It is not a *ci*, although it is a song. Its line-length is uneven, and its rhyme does not conform to poetic rules.

詩

漁		yú	to fish, a person who fishes, fisherman
歌		gē	song
子		zǐ	noun suffix
西		xī	west
塞		sài	fortress
山		shān	mountain
西塞山			place name (in modern Zhejiang Province)
前		qián	before, in front of
白		bái	white
鷺		lù	egret
飛		fēi	to fly
桃		táo	peach, peach tree
花		huā	flower, blossom
流		liú	to flow
水		shuǐ	water
鱖		guì	the mandarin fish
魚		yú	fish
肥		féi	fat

Continued ▶

青	qīng	dark green, dark
箬	ruò	bamboo (a type of broad-leaf bamboo used in making hats, mats, etc.)
笠	lì	bamboo hat
綠	lǜ	green
蓑	suō	straw rain cape
衣	yī	clothing
斜	xié	slanting, tilted, inclined
風	fēng	wind
細	xì	small, delicate
雨	yǔ	rain
不	bù	no, not
須	xū	to need
歸	guī	return

詩

塞下曲

林暗草驚風，將軍夜引弓。
平明尋白羽，沒在石棱中。

盧綸
Lú Lún

∞

Lu Lun is not a famous poet, but this is a famous poem. There are a number of passes or gates through the Great Wall. These are called sài (when used as a verb it is pronounced sè.). Xia here means inside the wall rather than below the wall.

The story refers to the tale told about the great Li Guang the "Flying General" in the Records of the Historian by Sima Qian (Ssu-ma Ch'ien).

General Li thought he saw a tiger in the night and shot an arrow at it. The following morning he found his arrow imbeded in a rock. He shot a second and third arrow at the rock but they wouldn't penetrate it.

Nowadays a *qu (ch'u)* is merely a note on the musical scale, but it used to be a poetic song, the style of versification most popular during the Yuan Dynasty.

塞	sài	fortress
下	xià	beneath, under, to descend (here inside the fortress)
曲	qǔ	a song, the qu poetic form (ch'ü)
林	lín	forest
暗	àn	dark
草	cǎo	grass (it produces)
驚	jīng	frightening (afraid)
風	fēng	wind, the grass frightens the wind
將	jiāng	to lead, a leader
軍	jūn	military, the army
將軍		general (here Li Guang of the Han Dynasty)
夜	yè	night
引	yǐn	to draw a bow
弓	gōng	bow
平	píng	level, just, peaceful
明	míng	bright, light
平明		early morning
尋	xún	look for (the general is looking for his arrow)
白	bái	white
羽	yǔ	feather, the feathers of his arrow

詩

沒	mò	to be hidden, out of view (the arrow entered a rock)
在	zài	at, in, on
石	shí	rock, stone
棱	léng	point, ridge
石棱		a jagged rock
中	zhōng	middle, in, within

塞下曲

月黑雁飛高，單于夜遁逃。
欲將輕騎逐，大雪滿弓刀。

盧綸
Lú Lún

∞

Lu Lun writes again on military affairs at the edge of empire. Both his poems in this collection bear the same title but his fame rests principally on this poem.

詩

塞	sài	fortress
下	xià	beneath, under, to descend
曲	qǔ	a song, a poem written in the *qu* style (ch'ü)
月	yuè	moon, month
黑	hēi	black, dark
雁	yàn	wild goose
飛	fēi	to fly
高	gāo	high, tall
單于	Chányú	a title, chieftain of the Xiong Nu tribe
夜	yè	night
遁	dùn	escape
逃	táo	flee
欲	yù	want (the Chinese general is the subject here. He wants to catch the Chanyu)
將	jiàng	to lead (troops)
輕	qīng	light (in weight)
騎	qí	to ride a horse
輕騎		light cavalry (abbreviations for 輕騎兵)
逐	zhú	catch up with, overtake

Continued ▶

大	dà	big, great
雪	xuě	snow
滿	mǎn	to fill, fill (here to cover)
弓	gōng	a bow
刀	dāo	knife
弓刀		weapons

詩

游子吟

慈母手中線，游子身上衣。
臨行密密縫，意恐遲遲歸。
誰言寸草心，報得三春暉。

孟郊
Mèng Jiāo

Meng Jiao had an unhappy life. After a promising beginning as a popular young intellectual, Meng failed the examinations. He eventually passed the exams only to be fired from the only post he ever obtained. Although Meng became an important poet, his life became that of an embittered, cynical hanger-on to his more successful friends. Meng's poetry frequently concentrates on the image of cold—cold weather, cold mountains, suffering from cold. A sad man, he wrote much sad poetry.

Here he longs to repay his mother's kindness but, recognizing the impossibility of doing so, he asks—can the tender grass ever repay the spring sunshine?

游	yóu	to travel, to swim
子	zǐ	noun suffix
游子		a traveler
吟	yín	a type of poem, a song poem
慈	cí	kind
母	mǔ	mother
手	shǒu	hand
中	zhōng	middle, in, within
線	xiàn	thread
游	yóu	to travel, to swim
子	zǐ	noun suffix
游子		a traveler
身	shēn	body
上	shàng	above, on, to ascend
衣	yī	clothing

詩

臨	lín	near, near to, close to
行	xíng	to go, depart
臨行		soon to depart
密密	mì	close, fine textured
縫	féng	to sew, to stitch, specifically a close, fine stitch resulting in a finely sewn garment (the verb *féng* 縫 would not be used to describe weaving or broad stitching. Here use of the word *féng* implies that his mother labored to make a tightly sewn garment that would keep her son warm)

意	yì	think, thought, idea
恐	kǒng	worry
遲遲	chí	late
歸	guī	return

誰	shuí	who
言	yán	say
寸	cùn	inch (Chinese inch)
草	cǎo	grass
寸草		fine or tender young grass
心	xīn	heart

Continued ▶

報	bào	to answer, to repay a favor or kindness
得	dé	can, be able
報得		to be able to repay
三	sān	three, third
春	chūn	spring
三春		the three months of spring, the spring season
暉	huī	sunlight

詩

觀獵

角鷹初下秋草稀，
鐵驄拋鞯去如飛。
少年獵得平原兔，
馬後橫稍意氣歸。

王昌齡
Wáng Chāngling

∞

Wang Changling is a well-known poet of the early Tang who is famous for his frontier poetry. He wrote few poems but they are highly regarded. During his life, his poetry was more popular than nearly all other Tang poets, and his poetic criticism was very influential. Not much is known about his life. He passed his imperial exams in 727, held several insignificant posts and died early in the An Lushan rebellion.

The poem simply celebrates hunting.

觀	guān	observe
獵	liè	hunt
角	jiǎo	corner, angle, horn (here a hood, the leather hood covering the eyes of a falcon before the bird is released to hun)
鷹	yīng	falcon, hawk, eagle
初	chū	first
下	xià	beneath, under, to descend
秋	qiū	autumn
草	cǎo	grass
稀	xī	sparse, rare
鐵	tiě	iron
驄	cōng	a piebald horse, a black and white spotted horse
鐵驄		a piebald horse (here the person riding the piebald horse)
拋	pāo	to throw
鞚	kòng	the reins
去	qù	go
如	rú	as, like
飛	fēi	fly

詩

少	shào	young (if third tone it means few)
年	nián	year
少年		a youth
獵	liè	to hunt
得	dé	obtain
平	píng	even, level
原	yuán	plain, prairie
兔	tù	rabbit
馬	mǎ	horse
後	hòu	after, later, empress, behind (here the rump or haunch of the horse)
橫	héng	sideways, crosswise, at right angles
意	yì	idea, feeling
氣	qì	air, disposition, energy
意氣		in high spirits
歸	guī	return

出塞

秦時明月漢時關，
萬里長征人未還。
但使盧城飛將在，
不教胡馬度陰山。

王昌齡
Wáng Chāngling

∞

Chu Sai 出塞 was a martial song popular during the Tang Dynasty. Wang Changling was famous for his frontier fortress poetry (*bian sai shi* 邊塞詩) during the westward expansion of the Tang Dynasty.

Here Wang writes that things don't change. The moon, passes and fortresses are still there. If the Flying General of Lucheng City were still alive he wouldn't have let the Hu tatars get through the Yin mountains into China. The poem is written as he is leaving the fortress to go fight the tatars.

詩

出	chū	come out, go out
塞	sài	fortress
秦	Qín	Qin Dynasty (Ch'in) (221-207 B.C.)
時	shí	time, at the time of
明	míng	bright
月	yuè	moon
漢	Hàn	Han Dynasty (206 B.C. - 220 A.D.)
時	shí	time, at the time of
關	guān	frontier pass
萬	wàn	ten thousand
里	lǐ	mile (a Chinese mile is equivalent to one-third of a modern English mile)
長	cháng	long
征	zhēng	bring into submission, campaign to bring into submission
人	rén	person
未	wèi	still not
還	huán	return

Continued ▶

但	dàn	only
使	shǐ	to cause, to render, if
但使		if only (if only the general had arrived…)
盧	lú	black, sound used to transliterate names
城	chéng	city
盧城		place name (Lucheng City in Hebei Province)
飛	fēi	to fly
將	jiàng	a general
飛將		"The Flying General" (a nickname for General Li Guang of the Western Han Dynasty)
在	zài	at, in, on, be there, exist
不	bú	no, not
教	jiào	allow, let (if first tone it means to teach)
胡	hú	name used for Tatar tribes (basic meaning is foolish)
馬	mǎ	horse
度	dù	to pass, cross over
陰	yīn	dark, secret
山	shān	mountain
陰山		place name (located in southern Mongolia)

詩

芙蓉樓送辛漸

寒雨連江夜入吳，
平明送客楚山孤。
洛陽親友如相問，
一片冰心在玉壺。

王昌齡
Wáng Chāngling

Usually in Chinese poetry, when one's heart is said to be "pure" it means loyal. The theme of loyalty appears frequently in the sense of loyalty to the Dynasty. Here however Wang Changling is reassuring his relatives and friends back in Luoyang of his loyalty to them. The poem also expresses Wang's tranquility and peace of mind.

芙	fú	hibiscus, lotus
蓉	róng	hibiscus
芙蓉		lotus
樓	lóu	multi-storied building
芙蓉樓		proper name (Fu Rong pavillion or Fu Rong tower)
送	sòng	send, send off
辛	xīn	piquant, difficult, a surname
漸	jiàn	gradually, to flow (here a person's name)
辛漸		a person's name (Mr. Xin Jian)
寒	hán	cold
雨	yǔ	rain
連	lián	connect, join
江	jiāng	river
夜	yè	night
入	rù	enter
吳	Wú	place name (old name for Jiangsu Province. Originally it was the major area of the Wu Kingdom of the Three Kingdoms)

詩

平	píng	flat
明	míng	bright
平明		early morning
送	sòng	send, send off, see off
客	kè	guest
楚	Chǔ	place name (old name for Hubei and also Hunan. An ancient state which existed 740-330 B.C.)
山	shān	mountain
孤	gū	alone ("I see the Chu mountains alone." His guest has left)
洛	Luò	place name (two tributaries of the Yellow River rising in Shaanxi)
陽	yáng	sun
洛陽		place name (city in Henan Province, capital of the Eastern Han Dynasty)
親	qīn	related, relatives
友	yǒu	friend
如	rú	as, similar to, if
相	xiāng	reciprocal, reciprocally
問	wèn	to ask

Continued ▶

一	yí	a, one
片	piàn	slice, flake
冰	bīng	ice
心	xīn	heart
在	zài	at, in, on
玉	yù	jade
壺	hú	pot, vessel, vase

詩

游春曲

萬樹江邊杏，新開一夜風。
滿園深淺色，照在綠波中。

王涯
Wáng Yá

∞

Wang Ya was a veteran Tang Dynasty official and relatively minor poet who wrote much in the Fu style. He earned his *jin shi* degree in 792 and held a number of positions. In the political factionalism between the palace eunuchs and the officials, Wang Ya took sides against a eunuch plot. The eunuchs triumphed, and in 835 Wang Ya was executed.

游	yóu	travel, drift, swim, float
春	chūn	spring
曲	qǔ	a *qu (ch'u)* or song poem
萬	wàn	ten thousand
樹	shù	tree (here used as a measure word for 杏 xìng, apricot trees)
江	jiāng	river
邊	biān	bank, shore
杏	xìng	apricots
新	xīn	new, newly
開	kāi	open
一	yí	a, one
夜	yè	night
風	fēng	wind
滿	mǎn	to fill, full
園	yuán	garden
深	shēn	deep
淺	qiǎn	shallow
色	sè	color
深淺色		dark and light colors

詩

照	zhào	shine, reflect (the blossoms reflecting on the river waves)
在	zài	at, in, on
綠	lǜ	green
波	bō	wave
中	zhōng	middle, in, within (in the midst of green waves)

調張籍

李杜文章在，光燄萬丈長。
不知群兒愚，那用故謗傷？
蚍蜉撼大樹，可笑不自量。

韓愈
Hán Yù

∞

Han Yu is one of China's most famous men of letters. Called the Prince of Literature, he is famous for the excellence of his writing, his advocacy of Confucianism and his leadership of the Ancient Style (*gu wen* 古文) neoclassical prose movement. Orphaned and impoverished as a child, Han Yu rose to become a leading statesman, essayist and poet. He was also a critic. His poems are like art or literary criticism.

By the late Tang, poetic tastes had changed to the extent that people ridiculed the earlier poets including Li Bai and Du Fu. In a poem written to Zhang Ji, Han Yu comes to their defense, pointedly wondering at the stupidity of the critics.

Above is the first six lines taken from the longer poem.

詩

調	tiào	ridicule (a person), to mock, scoff
張	Zhāng	surname
籍	jí	a population register, to register (here a given name)
張籍		proper name (Zhang Ji was a famous Tang Dynasty poet)
李	Lǐ	surname (here refers to Li Bai)
杜	Dù	surname (here refers to Du Fu)
文	wén	literature
章	zhāng	essay, document, chapter
文章		literary compositions
在	zài	at, in, on
光	guāng	bright, brightness
燄	yàn	flame
萬	wàn	ten thousand, many
丈	zhàng	measure word for length, ten feet
長	cháng	long, length
不	bù	no, not
知	zhī	know
群	qún	numerous, multitudes
兒	ér	child
愚	yú	stupid, foolish, silly ("(I) don't know why they're so stupid")

Continued ▶

那	nǎ	where, how
用	yòng	to use
那用		what's the use…
故	gù	old, ancient, a reason, cause, pretext (here to find an excuse)
謗	bàng	slander
傷	shāng	wound
蚍	pí	ant
蜉	fú	ant
蚍蜉		ant (note that mayi is the modern term for ant rather than pifu)
撼	hàn	shake
大	dà	large
樹	shù	tree ("an ant trying to shake a tree" is a Chinese metaphor for futility)
可	kě	be able
笑	xiào	laugh
可笑		laughable, ridiculous
不	bú	not, do not
自	zì	self
量	liáng	to measure
自量		estimate one's ability or strength

詩

楓橋夜泊

月落烏啼霜滿天，
江楓漁火對愁眠。
姑蘇城外寒山寺，
夜半鐘聲到客船。

張繼
Zhāng Jì

Zhang Ji was born in Hubei, passed his exams and had an official career. He attained high office, rising to secretary in the Board of Revenue. Although remembered more as a poet than a statesman, very few of his poems have come down to us. He is famous in particular for this poem with its melancholy images haunting the homesick poet's uneasy sleep.

楓	fēng	maple tree
橋	qiáo	bridge
夜	yè	night
泊	bó	to moor, to anchor a boat
月	yuè	moon, month
落	luò	to descend
烏	wū	crow
啼	tí	sound made by birds, caw, chirp, etc.
霜	shuāng	frost
滿	mǎn	to fill, full
天	tiān	sky, heaven
江	jiāng	river
楓	fēng	maple tree
漁	yú	to fish, one who fishes, a fisher, a fisherman
火	huǒ	fire (here the fires on the fishing boats)
對	duì	to face, to be opposite
愁	chóu	melancholy
眠	mián	to sleep

詩

姑	gū	aunt (sister of father)
蘇	sū	to revive
姑蘇		place name (old name for Suzhou)
城	chéng	city
外	wài	out, outside
寒	hán	cold
山	shān	mountain
寒山		place name (Han Mountain west of Suzhou)
寺	sì	temple
寒山寺		place name (the Han Shan Temple in Suzhou, now a popular tourist attraction)
夜	yè	night
半	bàn	half, mid
鐘	zhōng	bell
聲	shēng	sound
到	dào	to arrive
客	kè	guest (in Chinese poetry "guest" frequently means oneself)
船	chuán	boat

雨過山村

雨里雞鳴一兩家，
竹溪村路板橋斜。
婦姑相喚浴蠶去，
閑著中庭梔子花。

王建
Wáng Jiàn

Wang Jian is not famous and wrote few poems. His best known are palace poems but he also wrote poems with realistic themes. Wang had a long official career serving in both the court and the military.

In this poem *yù cán* 浴蠶 doesn't mean to wash silkworms in the sense of washing them clean. It refers to seed selection, the process of separating the best silkworms for future breeding purposes. Silkworms are put into water where the weak ones float to the surface. They are collected, boiled and made into silk. The strong silkworms are kept as breeding stock.

詩

雨	yǔ	rain
過	guò	pass through
山	shān	mountain
村	cūn	village
雨	yǔ	rain
里	lǐ	in
雞	jī	rooster, chicken
鳴	míng	to crow, sound made by chicken
一	yì	a, one
兩	liǎng	two
家	jiā	house, family, establishment
竹	zhú	bamboo
溪	xī	a stream (beside the stream are bamboo, so it is called *zhuxi*)
村	cūn	village
路	lù	road, a country road
板	bǎn	wooden board
橋	qiáo	bridge
斜	xiá	slanting, tilted, a slanting wooden bridge

Continued ▶

婦	fù	woman
姑	gū	aunt, mother-in-law, sister-in-law
婦姑		woman, a woman and her mother-in-law (it refers to two generations of women)
相	xiāng	reciprocal, each other, at me
喚	huàn	call
浴	yù	bathe, wash
蠶	cán	silkworm
去	qù	go
閑	xián	idle, leisure, barrier, trained
著	zhuó	to order, to place (auxiliary verb, participle)
閑著		to ignore, pay no attention
中	zhōng	middle, in, within
庭	tíng	court, courtyard
梔	zhī	jasmine
子	zǐ	noun suffix
花	huā	flower, blossom (nobody pays attention to the jasmine flowers in the courtyard)

詩

望洞庭

湖光秋月兩相和，
潭面無風鏡未磨。
遙望洞庭山水翠，
白銀盤里一青螺。

劉禹錫
Liú Yǔxī

Liu Yuxi had a turbulent political career during the Tang, enduring bouts of banishment and reinstatement. His poetry, written in a simple straightforward manner, was highly regarded. He can be considered an important poet. Folk elements and political allegory appear in much of his poetry. Many of his poems have come down to us.

望	wàng	look, peer
洞	dòng	a hole
庭	tíng	the court
湖	hú	lake
洞庭湖		place name (the famous Lake Dong Ting in Hunan Province)
光	guāng	light
秋	qiū	autumn
月	yuè	moon, month
兩	liǎng	two
相	xiāng	reciprocity, each other
和	hé	harmony
潭	tán	deep pond
面	miàn	surface
無	wú	haven't, without
風	fēng	wind
鏡	jìng	mirror
未	wèi	not yet
磨	mó	to polish, to rub ("the pond's surface without wind is like an unpolished mirror")

詩

遙	yáo	distance, distantly
望	wàng	look, peer
洞庭	dòngtíng	place name (the famous Lake Dong Ting in Hunan Province)
山	shān	mountain
水	shuǐ	water
山水		scenery, color
翠	cuì	green, color of jade
白	bái	white
銀	yín	silver
盤	pán	dish, plate
里	lǐ	in
一	yì	a, one
青	qīng	green
螺	luó	snail

烏衣巷

朱雀橋邊野草花，
烏衣巷口夕陽斜。
舊時王謝堂前燕，
飛入尋常百姓家。

劉禹錫
Liú Yǔxī

∞

Liu Yuxi grew up in Luoyang (Lo-yang), one of the centers of Chinese history. Here we see one of his recurring themes, melancholy reflections on history.

Red Sparrow Bridge was a famous bridge in Jinling City, the capital of the Eastern Jin (Chin) Dynasty. The Jin, mighty in its heyday during the fifth and sixth centuries, has become little more than wild grass. The mansions of important Jin officials lined the street nearby. Now swallows fly in and out of the dilapidated mansions which house mere commoners.

詩

烏	wū	black
衣	yī	clothing
巷	xiàng	a lane, alley
朱	zhū	red
雀	què	sparrow
橋	qiáo	bridge
邊	biān	side, beside
野	yě	wild
草	cǎo	grass
花	huā	flower, blossom
烏	wū	black
衣	yī	clothing
巷	xiàng	a lane, alley
口	kǒu	entrance, orifice
夕	xī	dusk
陽	yáng	sun
夕陽		setting sun
斜	xiá	slanting, tilted

Continued ▶

舊	jiù	old
時	shí	time, season
王	wáng	king, royal, surname (the powerful Wang family of the Six Dynasties period)
謝	xiè	thank, surname (the powerful Xie family. By the Tang Dynasty the two families had lost status)
堂	táng	a hall, main room of a house
前	qián	before
燕	yàn	the swallow
飛	fēi	to fly
入	rù	enter
尋	xún	look for, search
常	cháng	constantly, frequently, regular
尋常		ordinary
百	bǎi	hundred
姓	xìng	surname
百姓		the Chinese people, the common person
家	jiā	home, family, establishment

詩

暮江吟

一道殘陽鋪水中，
半江瑟瑟半江紅。
可憐九月初三夜，
露似珍珠月似弓。

白居易
Bái Jūyì

Bai Juyi is one of the most famous poets in Chinese literature, ranking just behind Li Bai and Du Fu. His name is also spelled Po Chu-i in Western sources, rendered in a different romanization and reflecting an earlier pronunciation. Bai was one of a number of reformers who rebelled against elaborate, artificial language in poetry. It is said that he would test the simplicity of his poems by reading them to a washer woman to make sure she understood them, consequently he became China's first poet to be popular among the common people.

Here the sun's rays reach out over half the river making the river appear half green and half red.

暮	mù	sunset
江	jiāng	river
吟	yín	chant, sing
一	yí	a, one
道	dào	road, path, line (here it is a measure word for the setting sun)
殘	cán	crescent, incomplete
陽	yáng	sun
鋪	pū	extend, spread
水	shuǐ	water (here river)
中	zhōng	middle, in, within
半	bàn	half, the sunlight spreads out over half the river
江	jiāng	river
瑟瑟	sè	turquoise
半	bàn	half, the sunlight spreads out over half the river
江	jiāng	river
紅	hóng	red

詩

可	kě	can, able
憐	lián	lovely
可憐		lovely (the modern meaning is to sympathize with, to pity)
九	jiǔ	nine, ninth
月	yuè	moon, month
初	chū	first, early
三	sān	three, third
初三		third day of the lunar month
夜	yè	night
露	lù	dew
似	sì	resemble
珍	zhēn	pearl, treasure, precious
珠	zhū	pearl
珍珠		pearl
月	yuè	moon, month
似	sì	resemble
弓	gōng	a bow

憶江南

江南好，
風景舊曾諳。
日出江花紅勝火，
春來江水綠如藍。
能不憶江南？

白居易
Bái Jūyì

Bai Juyi had a long, successful career as an official and an advisor to the court, serving through the reigns of eight emperors. He was a child prodigy in literature, got the *jin shi* degree when he was twenty-nine, and held numerous posts throughout the empire. He became a Han-Lin Scholar, a censor, Secretary of the Board of Punishments, and Governor of Henan, Suzhou and Hangzhou.

Bai wrote this poem in his old age in Luoyang, reminiscing about the south. The river in the poem is, as always, the Yangtze. This is a *ci (tz'u)* or lyric poem, originally set to music.

詩

憶	yì	remember, recollect
江	jiāng	river (here the Yangtze River)
南	nán	south
江	jiāng	river (here the Yangtze River)
南	nán	south
好	hǎo	good
風	fēng	wind
景	jǐng	scenery
風景		scenery
舊	jiù	old
曾	céng	ever, once
諳	ān	familiar
日	rì	sun, day
出	chū	come out, go out
江	jiāng	river (here the Yangtze River)
花	huā	flower, blossom
紅	hóng	red
勝	shèng	more than (here the flowers are redder than fire)
火	huǒ	fire

Continued ▶

春	chūn	spring
來	lái	come
江	jiāng	river (here the Yangtze River)
水	shuǐ	water
綠	lǜ	green
如	rú	compare to, such as
藍	lán	blue
能	néng	be able, can, can you…?
不	bú	no, not
憶	yì	remember, recollect
江	jiāng	river (here the Yangtze River)
南	nán	south

詩

草

離離原上草，一歲一枯榮。
野火燒不盡，春風吹又生。

白居易
Bái Jūyì

∞

There is an amusing story associated with this poem. When Bai Juyi was young he traveled to Chang'an to obtain the patronage of the famous poet Gu Kuang (725-814). Gu received Bai Juyi and made a pun on Bai's name using alternate meanings: bai—to get something for free, ju—to reside, and yi—easy. Gu Kuang quipped that although Bai Juyi's name implied that "without paying, living here is easy" Bai would soon find that it wasn't easy to live in Chang'an without paying. When Gu Kuang read the poems that Bai Juyi had brought he was so impressed that he agreed to sponsor the young poet. This poem is said to have been the first one that Bai Juyi showed to Gu. It is actually an eight-line lu shi, but most Chinese memorize only these first four lines, the most popular part of the poem.

草	cǎo	grass
離離	lí lí	to grow luxuriously (of grass and plants)
原	yuán	field, prairie
上	shàng	above, on, to ascend
草	cǎo	grass
一	yí	one
歲	suì	year
一	yì	one
枯	kū	wilt, wither, dry up
榮	róng	become green, oppose of wilt
野	yě	wild, the wilds, prairies
火	huǒ	fire
野火		wildfires, fires which occur naturally on the prairies
燒	shāo	to burn
不	bú	no, not
盡	jìn	consume, burn up
春	chūn	spring
風	fēng	wind
吹	chuī	blow
又	yòu	again
生	shēng	to produce, be born, life, living

憫農

春種一粒粟，秋收萬顆子。
四海無閒田，農夫猶餓死。

李紳
Lǐ Shēn

"Min Nong" was written by Li Shen, a lesser poet of the Tang. He was an outstanding scholar, as shown by his membership in the Han-Lin Academy, and had a long and distinguished official career.

Only several of his poems are remembered. This is the best known of them.

憫	mǐn	to synmpathize with
農	nóng	peasant, farmer
春	chūn	spring
種	zhòng	to plant
一	yí	one
粒	lì	a grain, a kernel
粟	sù	millet
秋	qiū	autumn
收	shōu	to receive, to collect, to harvest
萬	wàn	ten thousand, many
顆	kē	a kernel
子	zǐ	a seed, child, noun suffix
四	sì	four
海	hǎi	the sea
四海		the Four Seas, the entire world
無	wú	not have
閑	xián	fallow, empty, idle
田	tián	field

詩

農	nóng	farm, farming
夫	fū	a person, a laborer, an artisan
農夫		peasant
猶	yóu	still
餓	è	hunger
死	sǐ	die
餓死		to starve to death

鋤禾

鋤禾日當午，汗滴禾下土。
誰知盤中餐，粒粒皆辛苦。

李紳
Lǐ Shēn

∞

"Chu He" was written by Li Shen. You will recognize a sentiment similar to that of the poem "Min Nong" in this collection. Although himself a high official, Li Shen wrote sympathetically of the peasants who toil over their crops under a hot sun but still go hungry. Chinese children who don't finish eating their meal hear this poem recited to them. Parents scold that every grain of rice has cost someone backbreaking labor.

詩

鋤	chú	to cultivate, to weed, to hoe out or pull out weeds
禾	hé	standing grain, especially rice
鋤	chú	to cultivate, to weed, to hoe out or pull out weeds
禾	hé	standing grain, especially rice
日	rì	sun, day
當	dāng	just when, exactly at the time of
午	wǔ	noon
汗	hàn	sweat
滴	dī	drop, fall
禾	hé	rice, grain
下	xià	down, under, to descend (here to fall)
土	tǔ	earth
誰	shéi	who
知	zhī	know
盤	pán	plate, dish
中	zhōng	middle, in, within
餐	cān	food, meal

Continued ▶

粒粒	lì lì	a grain (of rice) (repeated for emphasis—every single grain!)
皆	jiē	all
辛	xīn	bitter, hard, suffering
苦	kǔ	bitter
辛苦		difficult, hard work

詩

江雪

千山鳥飛絕，萬徑人蹤滅。
孤舟簑笠翁，獨釣寒江雪。

柳宗元
Liǔ Zōngyuán

∞

Liu Zongyuan was a good poet and an even better essayist. He was active in the reform movement led by Han Yu to simplify the elaborate prose style then popular. Note the simplicity of this poem which makes it a favorite for memorization by school children. Note also the parallelism of the two couplets.

Liu suffered a political reverse which led to his banishment, first to Hunan, then later to distant Guizhou where he died. He produced his best writing while in exile.

This poem inspired a famous Song Dynasty painting.

Last Rays of the Setting Sun

江	jiāng	river
雪	xuě	snow
千	qiān	one thousand
山	shān	mountain
鳥	niǎo	bird
飛	fēi	fly
絕	jué	to cut short (here means discontinued. The birds have stopped flying because of the snow)
萬	wàn	ten thousand
徑	jìng	a road, a short cut, path, track
人	rén	person
蹤	zōng	a footprint
滅	miè	to destroy, to disappear (because the snow covered it)
孤	gū	alone
舟	zhōu	boat
簑	suō	straw rain cape
笠	lì	bamboo hat
翁	wēng	an old woman
獨	dú	alone
釣	diào	fishing, to fish
寒	hán	cold
江	jiāng	river
雪	xuě	snow

詩

尋隱者不遇

松下問童子，
言師采藥去。
只在此山中，
雲深不知處。

賈島
Jiǎ Dǎo

∞

Jia Dao was an eccentric Buddhist priest intensely devoted to the writing of poetry. One day in the street, deep in thought about whether to use the word "push" or "knock" in a poem, he was pushing and knocking the air with his hands when he accidentally assaulted the retinue of the great governor-poet Han Yu. Han Yu, a poet himself, understood Jia Dao's problem and suggested that he use the word "knock" in his poem. Han Yu took Jia under his protection. Thereafter Jia left the priesthood and attempted an official career with mixed results. An emperor exiled him because of his lampoons, but he was amnestied. Jia was given official positions but never took them. He used to write large quantities of poetry, then at the end of the year burn them, in reparation, he said, for the damage they had done to his mental powers.

尋	xún	search for
隱	yǐn	to cover, a recluse
者	zhě	one who…, that which…
隱者		a recluse
不	bú	no, not
遇	yù	to meet
松	sōng	pine tree
下	xià	beneath, under, to descend
問	wèn	ask
童	tóng	child
子	zǐ	noun suffix, child
童子		(here an apprentice or understudy. A young person who would live with the recluse and receive instruction in subjects such as religion, painting, calligraphy)
言	yán	to say
師	shī	master
采	cǎi	to pick, gather up, pluck
藥	yào	medicine, medicinal herbs (the master went out to pick medicinal herbs himself)
去	qù	go, depart

詩

只	zhǐ	only
在	zài	at, in, on
此	cǐ	this, here
山	shān	mountain
中	zhōng	middle, in, within
雲	yún	cloud
深	shēn	deep
不	bù	no, not
知	zhī	know
處	chù	a place (here, in a place I don't know)

雁門太守行

黑雲壓城城欲摧，
甲光向日金鱗開。
角聲滿天秋色里，
塞上燕脂凝夜紫。

李賀
Lǐ Hè

∞

The young and talented Li He was morbidly preoccupied with death and the passage of time. A brilliant scholar, he stood for his exam in Chang'an while still in his teens. Following a brief lifetime of chronic illness, Li died at twenty-six.

Li was highly eccentric. He would ride out on horseback, deep in thought, writing impressions on scraps of paper which he would toss into the air and which would be collected by a servant. In the evening Li would make the fragments into poetry.

Li shocked and repelled the literary establishment with his imagery of desolation, blood, ghosts and death. He was called the graveyard poet and the ghost poet, and is now sometimes compared to Baudelaire.

In this poem the governor of Yan Men walks in the province. When he departs it will be to go into battle, a battle which he will surely lose. There was a play based on this story.

詩

雁	yàn	wild goose
門	mén	gate, door
雁門		place name (name of a commandery in ancient China)
太	tài	great
守	shǒu	a governor
太守		governor (an official title in ancient China)
行	xíng	go, walk, do, act
黑	hēi	black, dark
雲	yún	cloud
壓	yā	press down, push down, weigh on
城	chéng	city
欲	yù	want, will, about to (be)
摧	cuī	destroy
甲	jiǎ	armour, the subject of the sentence
光	guāng	light, shine
向	xiàng	toward (here it means the armour is reflecting the sun)
日	rì	sun, day
金	jīn	gold
鱗	lín	a (fish) scale
開	kāi	open (here, the armour opens like fish scales)

Continued ▶

角	jiǎo	angle, corner, horn, bugle
聲	shēng	sound
滿	mǎn	fill, full, complete
天	tiān	heaven, sky
秋	qiū	autumn
色	sè	color (here the bugle sounds an autumn color)
里	lǐ	in
塞	sài	fortress
上	shàng	above, on, to ascend (here meaning at the site of the fortress, not actually on the fortress)
燕	yān	(bird) swallow (here an abbreviation for Yan Jing, the old name for Beijing or Peking)
脂	zhī	fat, tallow, rouge
燕脂		costmetic, rouge (it was made from fat. Peking cosmetics were famous in ancient China. Here the Peking rouge is a metaphor for the blood of the dead soldiers)
凝	níng	congeal, solidify
夜	yè	night
紫	zǐ	purple, like the purple color of night

詩

題都城南莊

去年今日此門中，
人面桃花相映紅。
人面不知何處去，
桃花依舊笑春風。

崔護
Cuī Hù

∞

Cui Hu is a hazy figure, a scholar official from Shandong Province. We don't know the dates of Cui's birth or death, but we do know he got his *jin shi* degree in 796. He also passed more difficult exams in 806 which would have meant promotion to high offices, but the record is not clear about which appointments he received. We are only told that Cui was made Chief Censor in 829, a very high post indeed.

On this day last year the poet saw a beautiful young woman standing by the door of her house, her face reflecting the blush of the peach blossoms.

題	tí	to inscribe
都	dū	the capital
門	mén	gate (here gate of a city)
南	nán	south
莊	zhuāng	village
去	qù	go
年	nián	year
去年		last year
今	jīn	now, present
日	rì	sun, day
今日		today
此	cǐ	this
門	mén	gate
中	zhōng	middle, in, within
人	rén	person
面	miàn	face
桃	táo	peach
花	huā	flower, blossom
相	xiāng	reciprocal, reciprocity, each other, at me
映	yìng	reflect
紅	hóng	red, reddish

詩

人面不知何處去	rén	person
	miàn	face
	bù	no, not
	zhī	know
	hé	what
	chù	place
	qù	go
桃花依舊	táo	peach
	huā	flower, blossom
	yī	follow, depend on
	jiù	old
依舊		as of old, like before
笑春風	xiào	laugh, smile
	chūn	spring
	fēng	wind

山行

遠上寒山石徑斜，
白雲生處有人家。
停車坐愛楓林晚，
霜葉紅于二月花。

杜牧
Dù Mù

∞

Du Mu is known as the Lesser Du *(Xiao Du)* in contradistinction to Du Fu who is known as the Greater Du *(Da Du)*. Du Mu was born into a scholarly family in Chang'an where his father was a distinguished statesman. Du Mu passed his *jin shi* examination and served in provincial posts but was repelled by the bureaucratic factionalism in court between the Niu and Li cliques. He turned away from politics and devoted himself to poetry, the enjoyment of night life and beautiful women.

Du Mu was evidently in the south. He writes about the flowers of the second month of spring.

詩

山	shān	mountain
行	xíng	go, walk
遠	yuǎn	far, distant
上	shàng	above, on, to ascend
寒	hán	cold
山	shān	mountain
石	shí	rock, stone
徑	jìng	byway, path
斜	xiá	slanting, tilted
白	bái	white
雲	yún	clouds
生	shēng	to produce, be born, life, living (here the place where the white clouds were born)
處	chù	place
有	yǒu	exist, to have
人	rén	person
家	jiā	home, family, establishment

Continued ▶

停	tíng	stop
車	chē	cart, vehicle
坐	zuò	sit, due to, because of
愛	ài	to like, enjoy
楓	fēng	maple tree
林	lín	forest
晚	wǎn	evening, dusk
霜	shuāng	frost
葉	yè	leaf
紅	hóng	red
于	yú	more than
二	èr	two, second
月	yuè	moon, month
花	huā	flower, blossom

詩

赤壁

折戟沉沙鐵未銷，
自將磨洗認前朝。
東風不與周郎便，
銅雀春深鎖二喬。

杜牧
Dù Mù

∞

This poem is a political metaphor based on the great naval battle on the Yangtze at Red Cliffs, Hubei, early in the third century. The infamous General Cao Cao (Ts'ao Ts'ao) was defeated by Zhou Yu and Zhuge Liang through a stratagem. General Cao Cao's troops were seasick. Zhou sent a spy to suggest lashing the ships together so they wouldn't rock. When Cao Cao had done so, Zhou started a fire and Zhuge Liang used Taoist magic to make the wind blow the fire through the fleet, destroying it.

Du Mu concedes that Zhou Yu won the battle because he was clever, but if Zhou hadn't had the wind on his side he wouldn't have won. Du Mu laments that he doesn't have the powerful east wind (the support of the court) on his side.

LAST RAYS OF THE SETTING SUN

赤	chì	red
壁	bì	wall
赤壁		place name (located in Hubei on the Yangtze River)
折	zhé	broken
戟	jǐ	halberd, battle axe (here a metal axehead from the Three Kingdoms period (A.D. 221-265))
沉	chén	to settle, trickle down (here to sink into the sand)
沙	shā	sand
鐵	tiě	iron
未	wèi	not yet
銷	xiāo	disappear
自	zì	self
將	jiāng	take
磨	mó	grind, rub
洗	xǐ	wash
認	rèn	know, understand, to recognize
前	qián	before, previous, in front of
朝	cháo	dynasty ("after I was it I recognize it as being from a previous dynasty")

詩

東	dōng	east
風	fēng	wind (east wind here symbolizing the support of a powerful patron)
不	bù	no, not
與	yǔ	give, make
周	Zhōu	a surname
郎	láng	ancient official title
周郎		proper name (General Zhou Yu. His official title was Zhong Lang Jiang which people shortened to Lang, thus he bacame known as Zhou Lang)
便	biàn	easy, to make it easy
銅	tóng	copper
雀	què	sparrow (*tongque* means the Copper Sparrow Pavillion of Cao Cao)
春	chūn	spring (also a metaphor for man-woman relations and illicit relationships)
深	shēn	deep (here late spring)
鎖	suǒ	to lock, lock up
二	èr	two
喬	Qiáo	a surname
二喬		the two Qiao sisters (had Zhou Yu lost, Cao Cao would have forced the Qiao sisters to live with him in his Copper Sparrow Pavilion. Da Qiao and Xiao Qiao, two of the many beautiful women of the Three Kingdoms Period. An added reason for Zhou Yu to win was the potential loss of his wife who was one of the Qiao sisters to live with him in his Copper Sparrow Pavillion)

泊秦淮

煙籠寒水月籠沙，
夜泊秦淮近酒家。
商女不知亡國恨，
隔江猶唱後庭花！

杜牧
Dù Mù

This poem is also a political allegory, as Du Mu compares the cabaret singing girl to officials of the imperial court. The Tang Dynasty is in decline and will become extinct, but the singing girl is blissfully unaware of this. Du Mu, in his boat, listens to the girl's song float across the river.

詩

泊	bó	to anchor, to moor, to dock at
秦	Qín	proper name (Qin Dynasty. Surname. Alternate name for Shaanxi Province)
淮	Huái	place name (Huai River)
秦淮		place name (Qin Huai River in Nanjing)
煙	yān	smoke, haze
籠	lǒng	to cover, to blanket
寒	hán	cold
水	shuǐ	water (here water of the Qin Huai River)
月	yuè	moon, month
籠	lǒng	to cover, to blanket
沙	shā	sand ("white moonlight shines on the white sand (of the riverbank)")
夜	yè	night
泊	bó	to anchor, to moor, to dock at
秦	Qín	proper name (Ch'in Dynasty. Surname. Alternate name for Shaanxi Province)
淮	Huái	place name (Huai River)
秦淮		place name (Qin Huai River in Nanjing)
近	jìn	near, getting close to
酒	jiǔ	wine
家	jiā	establishment, home, family
酒家		a tavern, cabaret, wine shop

Continued ▶

商	shāng	commerce
女	nǚ	woman, girl
商女		a singing girl, young woman who earns a living by singing in taverns
不	bù	no, not
知	zhī	know
亡	wáng	die, perish
國	guó	state, country
亡國		an extinct country, a nation which has ceased to exist
恨	hèn	remorse, regret (the singing girl doesn't know the sorrow of having her country perish (In modern Chinese *hen* means to hate))
隔	gé	separated (here separated by the river. The poet is in a boat on the opposite side of the river from the tavern)
江	jiāng	river
猶	yóu	still
唱	chàng	sing
後	hòu	back, rear
庭	tíng	courtyard
花	huā	flower, blossom
後庭花		a song title (the title of the song the cabaret girl is singing. According to tradition, a king who loved this song lost his kingdom, therefore people called it "The Song of a Lost Country". It was composed by the last emperor of the Chen Dynasty)

秋夕

銀燭秋光冷畫屏，
輕羅小扇撲流螢。
天階夜色涼如水，
臥看牽牛織女星。

杜牧
Dù Mù

Du Mu portrays a young concubine in the Imperial harem. Her story is interwoven with the legend of separated lovers, that of the Herd Boy and the Weaver Girl. The boy and girl, represented by two stars separated by the Milky Way, meet only once a year, on the seventh day of the seventh month. The lovers cross a bridge formed by magpies, but at dawn they part.

Fans, due to their shape, allude to the moon, and the moon is frequently a metaphor for deserted women. This poem however, also has a frolicsome tone to it. Occasionally the imperial concubines were given time off to enjoy themselves--they could do whatever they wanted. Here she playfully bats at fireflies and dreams of romance.

秋	qiū	autumn
夕	xī	night, evening
銀	yín	silver
燭	zhú	candle
秋	qiū	autumn
光	guāng	light
冷	lěng	cold (here to cause to be cold)
畫	huà	a painting
屏	píng	a screen
畫屏		a decorative painted screen
輕	qīng	light (of low weight)
羅	luó	silk
小	xiǎo	little
扇	shàn	a fan
撲	pū	to swat
流	liú	flow, drift, float
螢	yíng	firefly

詩

天	tiān	sky, heaven (here it should be translated celestial: it is used as an honorific adjective modifying steps. We are thereby informed that these are steps of the imperial palace)
階	jiē	steps
夜	yè	night
色	sè	color, scenery
涼	liáng	cool
如	rú	like, resembling
水	shuǐ	water
臥	wò	to recline
看	kàn	to look
牽	qiān	lead by a leash, to pull along
牛	niú	an ox
牽牛		the Herd Boy star (the star Altair)
織	zhī	to weave
女	nǚ	female
星	xīng	a star
織女星		the Weaver Girl star (the star Vega in the constellation Lyra)

過華清宮

長安回望繡成堆，
山頂千門次第開。
一騎紅塵妃子笑，
無人知是荔枝來。

杜牧
Dù Mù

This poem satirizes the decadence of the court of Emperor Xuan Zong. An official courier rides in desperate haste to the court. No one knows that the courier is merely bringing lychee fruits to the emperor's concubine.

The Hua Qing palace no longer exists. Now the area is called Hua Qing Ji. There is a hot spring were the concubine Yang Guifei bathed. The area has become a tourist attraction near modern Xi'an.

詩

過	guò	to pass
華	huá	China, splendid, magnificent
清	qīng	bright, clear, quiet
宮	gōng	palace
華清宮		proper name (a palace near Chang'an)
長	cháng	long
安	ān	peace
長安		place name (Chang'an, capital of the Tang. Modem Xi'an)
回	huí	return
望	wàng	to view, look toward
回望		to look back
繡	xiù	to embroider
成	chéng	to become
堆	duī	to pile, a pile
山	shān	mountain
頂	dǐng	top
千	qiān	thousand
門	mén	door, gate
次	cì	a time, a series
第	dì	a senes, a sequence
次第		one by one
開	kāi	open

一	yí	one, a
騎	jì	rider and horse (if pronounced qí it means to ride)
紅	hóng	red
塵	chén	dust
妃	fēi	concubine
子	zǐ	noun suffix, child
妃子		a concubine (here it refers to Yang Guifei)
笑	xiào	laugh, smile
無	wú	not have
人	rén	person
無人		no one
知	zhī	know
是	shì	to be
荔	lì	lychee fruit
枝	zhī	branch
荔枝		lychee fruit
來	lái	come
		(lychee fruits don't last three days. The emperor sent a courier daily to bring lychee to the famous Yang Guifei)

詩

清明

清明時節雨紛紛，
路上行人欲斷魂。
借問酒家何處有，
牧童遙指杏花村。

杜牧
Dù Mù

This poem is entitled "Qing Ming", or "Pure Brightness". Qing Ming is Chinese memorial day, the 108th day after *Dongzhi* 冬至, the fifth of the twenty-four lunar periods. On this day the Chinese go to the cemetery to clean and tend the graves of relatives and ancestors. A memorial service is held which includes offerings of food, personal items, and the burning of paper money and incense.

Du Mu, traveling in distant parts, realizes that there is no one at home to tend to the graves of his family on this solemn day. He asks the whereabouts of a tavern to get out of the rain and reflect on his sadness.

清	qīng	pure
明	míng	bright
清明		pure brightness (fifth solar term) (Chinese memorial day. The third day of the third month)
清	qīng	pure
明	míng	bright
清明		pure brightness (fifth solar term) (Chinese memorial day. The third day of the third month)
時	shí	time
節	jié	division of time, term, festival
時節		at the time of
雨	yǔ	rain
紛	fēn	confused, disorderly, mixed
紛紛		pell mell, in confusion
路	lù	road
上	shàng	above, on, to ascend
行	xíng	walk, travel, do, act
人	rén	person
行人		traveller
欲	yù	want, will, soon will
斷	duàn	cut, break
魂	hún	spirit, mood
斷魂		depressed, sad (literally broken in spirit)

詩

借	jiè	to trouble someone, to importune (literally to borrow)
問	wèn	ask
借問		may I bother you to ask (same as the modern "*qǐngwèn*")
酒	jiǔ	wine
家	jiā	an establishment, home, family
酒家		a tavern, a place to sit, eat and drink, a wine shop
何	hé	what
處	chù	place
有	yǒu	exist, there is, there are
何處有		where is a
牧	mù	to tend animals, to herd animals, to herd cattle
童	tóng	a child
牧童		cow-boy, a real cowboy, a peasant boy riding a water buffalo (this is a job commonly given to an older child on Chinese farms)
遙	yáo	far, distant
指	zhǐ	point
杏	xìng	apricot
花	huā	flower, blossom
村	cūn	village
杏花村		Apricot Blossom Village (the village is famous for its wine-making)

夜雨寄北

君問歸期未有期，
巴山夜雨漲秋池。
何當共剪西窗燭，
卻話巴山夜雨時。

李商隱
Lǐ Shāngyǐn

∞

Li Shangyin is one of principal poets of the late Tang Dynasty and a major poet in China's literary history. He was the best-known poet of his day. Poets of the Song Dynasty were inspired to form a poetic school modeled on his style.

Li writes difficult poetry; mystical, obscure, abstruse, attempting the innovative phrase, the colorful word. But he is most closely associated with romantic poems. Traditionally, romance was not considered an appropriate subject for literature. In the late Tang however, romantic poetry became commonplace, and foremost among the amatory poets was Li Shangyin. He wrote extensively of romantic love, including love for his wife. Here Li, who is located in Ba in the south, writes a letter to his wife, asking—when can they stay up all night and talk about the time when it rained all night in the mountains of Ba?

詩

夜	yè	night
雨	yǔ	rain
寄	jì	to send, send a letter
北	běi	north
君	jūn	you, sir, you, madam, please…
問	wèn	ask
歸	guī	return
期	qī	a period of time, a date
未	wèi	not yet
有	yǒu	exist, to have
未有期		The time has not yet come when
巴	Bā	place name (Ba Province, in modern Sichuan)
山	shān	mountain
夜	yè	night
雨	yǔ	rain
漲	zhǎng	overflow, inundate, to rise, to flood
秋	qiū	autumn
池	chí	pool

Continued ▶

何	hé	what, how, when
當	dāng	should, to occupy a post, do, in, at
共	gòng	together
剪	jiǎn	cut
西	xī	west
窗	chuāng	window
燭	zhú	candle ("to cut (the wick of) a candle" is a conventional phrase meaning to stay up all night in conversation with a friend)
卻	què	but, yet, still
話	huà	talk
巴	Bā	place name (Ba Province, in modern Sichuan)
山	shān	mountain
夜	yè	night
雨	yǔ	rain
時	shí	time, the time when

詩

韓冬郎既席為詩相送因成二絕

十歲裁詩走馬成，
冷灰殘燭動離情。
桐花萬里丹山路，
雛鳳清于老鳳聲。

李商隱
Lǐ Shāngyǐn

∞

Although ranked below Li Bai or Du Fu, Li Shangyin is a major Tang Dynasty poet. The Chinese call the great Li Bai and Du Fu "Li-Du". Li Shangyin and Du Mu are called "Little Li-Du" *(Xiao Li-Du)*.

Li Shangyin has written this poem in the festive air of a going-away party being held in his honor. In the mood of fellowship of the occasion, he praises a poem written by his ten year old nephew. In China it is a compliment to refer to someone as a dragon or a phoenix, both marvelous and lucky creatures. Li flatters his brother-in-law, the boy's father, saying that the sound (poem) written by the young phoenix (the boy) is better than that written by the old phoenix (the boy's father).

雛	chú	young chick
鳳	fèng	phoenix
清	qīng	clear
于	yú	than (used in comparisons)
老	lǎo	old
鳳	fèng	phoenix
聲	shēng	sound
十	shí	ten
歲	suì	age, years old
裁	cái	to tailor, to fabricate (here to tailor a poem)
詩	shī	poetry
走	zǒu	run, gallop
馬	mǎ	horse
走馬		quickly, at the galloping of a horse (used adverbially)
成	chéng	complete, finish (he finishes the poem very quickly)

詩

冷	lěng	cold
灰	huī	ash (the cold ash of the burned candle wick. To speak of candlewick ashes or cutting a candle wick are conventional ways of saying that one stays up all night in conversation with a friend)
殘	cán	incomplete, remnant, injure, cut off
燭	zhú	candle
動	dòng	move, moving (experience), touched
離	lí	leave, depart
情	qíng	feeling, emotion
桐	tóng	paulowina tree, tung tree (a word used to describe a variety of trees. The phoenix will only alight in a Tong tree, thus implying that the boy is a phoenix)
花	huā	flower, blossom
萬	wàn	ten thousand
里	lǐ	mile (a Chinese mile is equivalent to one-third of a modern English mile)
丹	dān	red
山	shān	mountain
丹山		proper name (mythological mountain where phoenixes live)
路	lù	road (the boy has the road before him. He has before him the 10,000 *li* road leading to Dan Shan, again a reference to the phoenix)

Continued ▶

雛	chú	young
鳳	fèng	phoenix
清	qīng	clear
于	yú	than (used in comparisons)
老	lǎo	old
鳳	fèng	phoenix
聲	shēng	sound

詩

樂游原

向晚意不適，驅車登古原。
夕陽無限好，只是近黃昏。

李商隱
Lǐ Shāngyǐn

∞

Li Shangyin had an unsuccessful career. There were two cliques at court, the Li and the Niu, named after their premiers. Li Shangyin allied with one or the other of them occasionally but belonged to neither. Consequently he alienated both cliques and never attained a high position.

Li lived toward the end of the Tang. In this poem the sun is setting for both him and the dynasty.

Le You Yuan is a scenic spot in suburban Xi'an.

樂	lè	happy, joyful
游	yóu	swim, wander, roving
原	yuán	plain, prairie (here it is used as part of the place name *Le You Yuan*, which is a hill with a plateau on top)
樂游原		place name (located in Chang'an (modern Xi'an))
向	xiàng	near(ly) (today we would say *bàng* 傍 rather than xiàng)
晚	wǎn	evening
意	yì	feeling
不	bú	no, not
適	shì	comfortable
驅	qū	to drive
車	chē	chariot
登	dēng	to climb
古	gǔ	ancient
原	yuán	plateau, the Le You plateau (he drove his chariot up onto the plateau)

詩

夕	xī	evening
陽	yáng	sun
無	wú	not have
限	xiàn	limit
無限		limitless, extremely
好	hǎo	good
只	zhǐ	only
是	shì	to be, is
近	jìn	near, close to
黃	huáng	yellow
昏	hūn	dusk

傷田家

二月賣新絲，五月糶新谷；
醫得眼前瘡，剜卻心頭肉！

聶夷中
Niè Yízhōng

∞

Nie Yizhong came from a poor family in Shanxi Province. He got his *jin shi* degree in 871 and later held office. Writing mostly in the 5-character style, Nie was known for his bitingly sarcastic social commentary.

Notice the months during which activity occurrs in this poem. Silk is not harvested in the second month, nor is rice harvested in the fifth month. The impoverished peasants are selling their crops ahead of time out of desperation.

Not only will they be paid less for the immature silk and rice, but when harvest time comes they will have nothing left to sell.

There is a four-character phrase that describes the situation; *wān ròu bǔ chuāng* 剜肉補瘡 to cut out a piece of one's flesh in order to cure a boil. In other words, resort to a remedy that is worse than the ailment. Nie Yizhong is famous for this single poem.

詩

傷	shāng	feel sad, sympathize with
田	tián	field
家	jiā	home, family, establishment
田家		peasant's house
二	èr	two, second
月	yuè	moon, month
賣	mài	to sell
新	xīn	new
絲	sī	silk
五	wǔ	five, fifth
月	yuè	moon, month
糶	tiào	to sell (grain)
新	xīn	new
谷	gǔ	grain, rice
醫	yī	to treat an illness
得	dé	obtain
醫得		to get medical treatment for
眼	yǎn	eyes
前	qián	before, in front
眼前		the present
瘡	chuāng	skin ulcer, sore

Continued ▶

剜	wān	to cut out
卻	què	remove
心	xīn	heart
頭	tóu	head (here a noun suffix)
心頭		heart
肉	ròu	flesh, meat

詩

江鷗

白鳥波上棲，見人懶飛起。
爲有求魚心，不是戀江水。

崔道融
Cuī Dàoróng

Cui Daorong is quite famous, although little is known about his life.

The gulls didn't come here for the river water, they came here for the fish.

江	jiāng	river
鷗	ōu	gull
白	bái	white
鳥	niǎo	bird
波	bō	wave, ripple
上	shàng	above, an, to ascend
棲	qī	to perch, to stay
見	jiàn	see
人	rén	person
懶	lǎn	lazy, sluggish, reluctantly
飛	fēi	to fly
起	qǐ	arise
爲	wèi	because of
有	yǒu	have
求	qiú	seek
魚	yú	fish
心	xīn	heart (here thought)
不	bú	no, not
是	shì	to be
戀	liàn	be fond of, feel attached to, love
江	jiāng	river
水	shuǐ	water

詩

流水

流水在山澗，其小才如帶。
忽然成江河，因與它水會。
萬事皆如此，由小而及大。
小惡慎莫爲，終當受其害。

無名氏
Anonymous

An anonymous Tang poet offers a bit of homey morality.

流	liú	flow
水	shuǐ	water
流	liú	flow
水	shuǐ	water
在	zài	at, in, on
山	shān	mountain
澗	jiàn	crevasse, gorge, ravine
其	qí	possessive, his, hers, its, their, this, that
小	xiǎo	small
才	cái	only then, just then
如	rú	like
帶	dài	belt, ribbon
忽	hū	sudden
然	rán	adverbial particle, -ly, certainly, but, although, so, this
成	chéng	to become, to complete
江	jiāng	river
河	hé	river
江河		river

詩

因	yīn	because, a reason, a cause
與	yǔ	with
它	tā	other
水	shuǐ	water, stream
會	huì	meet, meeting (here a confluence with other rivers)
萬	wàn	ten thousand
事	shì	matters
皆	jiē	all
如	rú	like
此	cǐ	this
由	yóu	from
小	xiǎo	small
而	ér	thus, thereby, and
及	jí	to reach, extend, to attain
大	dà	large

Continued ▶

小	xiǎo	small
惡	è	evil
慎	shèn	caution, careful
莫	mò	don't
爲	wéi	to be, to act, to do
終	zhōng	to the end, finally
當	dāng	must
受	shòu	receive
其	qí	possessive, his, hers, its, their, this, that
害	hài	injury

詩

江上漁者

江上往來人，但愛鱸魚美。
君看一葉舟，出沒風波里。

范仲淹
Fàn Zhòngyān

∞

Fan Zhongyan was a well-known scholar-official of the Northern Song Dynasty. He rose to high office, fell from power, and was banished only to be recalled to service when the tatars invaded. He resoundingly defeated them and earned a heroic reputation. Chinese history judges Song Dynasty officials as loyal (*zhōng chén* 忠臣) or disloyal (*jiān chén* 奸臣) based on their willingness to resist the barbarian invasion. It is said of Fan that because of his loyalty he was among the first to suffer hardship and the last to enjoy happiness. His poetry appears in school textbooks.

江	jiāng	river
上	shàng	above, on, to ascend
漁	yú	fishing
者	zhě	one who, that which, -er
漁者		one who fishes, a fisher
江	jiāng	river
上	shàng	above, on, to ascend
往	wǎng	go
來	lái	come
往來		to go back and forth
人	rén	person
但	dàn	only
愛	ài	like
鱸	lú	a perch fish
魚	yú	fish
鱸魚		the perch, famous in China (This fish lives only in certain places in the Yangtze and cannot be transplanted to other places and survive)
美	měi	beautiful (here beautiful tasting, delicious)

詩

君	jūn	gentleman ("You, sir…", "Please…")
看	kàn	look, look at
一	yí	one, a
葉	yè	leaf
舟	zhōu	boat
出	chū	come out, go out (here to appear)
沒	mò	not, not existing (here to dissapear)
風	fēng	wind
波	bō	a wave
風波		storm (here it has a political meaning. The dynasty, like the leaf, was being swept helplessly along by events)
里	lǐ	in, inside (here inside the country)

泊船瓜洲

京口瓜洲一水間，
鍾山只隔數重山。
春風又綠江南岸，
明月何時照我還？

王安石
Wáng Ānshí

Wang Anshi was a prominent poet and essayist but was best known as a statesman and reformist politician. An excellent student, he passed his *jin shi* examination and distinguished himself in a number of posts. Upon promotion to State Councillor he initiated a program of sweeping reforms based on his own interpretations of the classics. Encompassing government, education, army, finance, law, Wang's radical reform movement touched nearly every aspect of life. The enormous controversey that resulted shaped much of the intellectual and political activity of the eleventh century.

詩

泊	bó	to anchor, to moor
船	chuán	boat
瓜	guā	melon
洲	zhōu	a geographical region
瓜洲		place name (opposite modern Zhenjiang city in Jiangsu Province)
京	jīng	capital
口	kǒu	orifice, opening
京口		place name (old name for Zhenjiang)
瓜	guā	melon
洲	zhōu	a geographical region
瓜洲		place name (opposite modern Zhenjiang city in Jiangsu Province)
一	yì	one, a
水	shuǐ	water (here a river, the Yangtze River)
間	jiān	in between (here between Jing Kou and Gua Zhou)

Continued ▶

鍾	zhōng	bell
山	shān	mountain
鍾山		place name (Zhongshan Mountain in Nanjing)
只	zhǐ	only
隔	gé	to separate, separate (here "Jing Kou and Gua Zhou are separated from Zhongshan by...")
數	shù	several
重	chóng	repeat (here a layer)
山	shān	mountain
春	chūn	spring
風	fēng	wind
又	yòu	again
綠	lǜ	green, cause to be green, to bring to life
江	jiāng	river
南	nán	south
岸	àn	bank, shore
明	míng	bright
月	yuè	moon, month
何	hé	what
時	shí	time
照	zhào	shine on
我	wǒ	I, me, my
還	huán	return

詩

梅花

牆角數枝梅，凌寒獨自開。
遙知不是雪，爲有暗香來。

王安石
Wáng Ānshí

∞

Wang Anshi's reform program led to decades of political controversey. Wang defended his program against some of the most brilliant and powerful statesmen of the day. In this poem he compares himself to plum blossoms which open early in the spring to defy the cruel cold and snow.

To the Chinese, the plum tree symbolizes the scholar, and a noble spirit. A plum blossom represents perseverence.

梅	méi	plum
花	huā	flower, blossom
牆	qiáng	wall
角	jiǎo	angle, corner
數	shù	number, numerous
枝	zhī	branch
梅	méi	plum
凌	líng	ice, to rise, aspire, confront, offend
寒	hán	cold
凌寒		to stand against the extreme cold
獨	dú	alone
自	zì	self
開	kāi	open (here, the blossoms open)
遙	yáo	distance, distantly
知	zhī	know
不	bú	no, not
是	shì	to be, is
雪	xuě	snow

詩

爲	wèi	because, for
有	yǒu	have, exist
暗	àn	dark, secret, dim
香	xiāng	frangrance
來	lái	come (because they have exuded their fragrance secretly)

春日偶成

雲淡風輕近午天，
傍花隨柳過前川。
時人不識余心樂，
將謂偷閑學少年。

程顥
Chéng Hào

Cheng Hao and his brother Cheng Yi became famous as the scholar-philosophers who influenced Zhu Xi, the progenitor of Neo-Confucianism.

Cheng was a precocious student. He passed his exams and served first as a magistrate and later a Censor. Cheng's father had ruined his career in futile opposition to the powerful reformer Wang Anshi, and to avoid the same fate Cheng took provincial posts away from conflict. He retired in his 40's to his birthplace Luoyang, and devoted himself to teaching and scholarly pursuits.

詩

春	chūn	spring
日	rì	sun, day
偶	ǒu	occasionally
成	chéng	complete
雲	yún	cloud
淡	dàn	pale, light in color
風	fēng	wind
輕	qīng	light, light in weight
近	jìn	near
午	wǔ	noon
天	tiān	day
傍	bàng	near to
花	huā	flower, blossom
隨	suí	follow
柳	liǔ	willow tree
過	guò	to pass
前	qián	before, in front of
川	chuān	riverbank, plain

Continued ▶

時	shí	time
人	rén	person
時人		other people
不	bù	no not
識	shí	recognize, understand
余	yú	I, my, mine
心	xīn	heart
樂	lè	happy
將	jiāng	to take, possibly, and then, thus
謂	wèi	say
偷	tōu	steal
閑	xián	leisure
偷閑		to idle, to loaf
學	xué	learn, imitate (applied to young people)
少	shào	young (read 4th tone it means young, read 3rd tone it means few)
年	nián	year
少年		youth

詩

題西林壁

橫看成嶺側成峰，
遠近高低各不同。
不識廬山真面目，
只緣身在此山中。

蘇軾
Sū Shì

∞

Su Shi is not only the pre-eminent poet of the Northern Song, but also a great painter, essayist and calligrapher. The Chinese refer to the Eight Great Prose Masters of the Tang and Song (*Tang Sung Ba Da Jia* 唐宋八大家). Two are Tang, six are Song. Of those six, three are from the Su family; Su Shi, his father Su Xun and his brother Su Zhe.

Xi Lin is the name of a temple. The verb *ti* 題 means to write an inscription on a wall with a brush. In ancient China, as today, it was the custom to write poetry on a folding fan, on the wall of a temple or on the wall of a friend's house.

題	tí	write a poem or inscription on a wall with a brush
西	xī	west
林	lín	woods, forest
西林		proper name (the name of a temple on Lushan, Mount Lu, Jiangxi province)
壁	bì	wall
橫	héng	horizontal
看	kàn	look at
橫看		look at something horizontally, to view it straight on, from the front
成	chéng	to become
嶺	lǐng	mountain range, ridge
側	cè	(look at) sideways, lengthwise
成	chéng	to become
峰	fēng	mountain peak, viewed from the side it looks like a mountain peak
遠	yuǎn	far, afar (when viewing Mt. Lu from afar)
近	jìn	near, close (when viewing Mt. Lu closeup)
高	gāo	high, tall (when viewing Mt. Lu from a high vantage point)
低	dī	low (when viewing Mt. Lu from a low vantage point)
各	gè	each
不	bù	no, not
同	tóng	same

詩

不	bù	no, not
識	shí	know
廬	Lú	place name
山	shān	mountain
廬山		Mt. Lu
真	zhēn	real
面	miàn	face, appearance
目	mù	eye
面目		face (of Mt. Lu)
只	zhǐ	only
緣	yuán	reason, cause, because of
只緣		only this reason…, the reason is…
身	shēn	body, one's body, you, oneself
在	zài	at, in, on
此	cǐ	this
山	shān	mountain
中	zhōng	middle, in, within

飲湖上初晴後雨

水光瀲灩晴方好，
山色空濛雨亦奇。
欲把西湖比西子，
淡妝濃抹總相宜。

蘇軾
Sū Shì

∞

Su Shi, or Su Dongpo 蘇東坡 as he was known by his assumed name *hao* 號, is one of the most brilliant figures in Chinese literature. Su was a master of both *shi* and *ci* styles of poetry and wrote the best *ci* poetry of the Song Dynasty. His calligraphy was also superb. The Song has four famous calligraphers, and Su ranks first.

Su Shi wrote this poem while drinking on a lake, watching the weather change from sunny to rainy. Su compares the scenery to a woman, the beauty Xi Shi. The beauty of both the scenery and the woman are exquisite, whether adorned or in their natural states.

詩

飲	yǐn	to drink
湖	hú	lake
上	shàng	above, on, to ascend
初	chū	the beginning, the first
晴	qíng	fine, clear, weather clearing up
後	hòu	after, behind
雨	yǔ	rain
水	shuǐ	water
光	guāng	light
瀲灩	liànyàn	shimmering reflected light
晴	qíng	fine, clear, weather clearing up
方	fāng	only then
好	hǎo	beautiful
山	shān	mountain
色	sè	color, scenery
空	kōng	empty
濛	méng	mist
空濛		shifting, changing mist
雨	yǔ	rain
亦	yì	and, moreover
奇	qí	strange, wondrous

Continued ▶

欲	yù	to want
把	bǎ	to take, to put
西	xī	west
湖	hú	lake
西湖		West Lake, Hangzhou
比	bǐ	compare
西	xī	west
子	zǐ	child, noun suffix
西子		a beautiful woman of the Spring and Autumn Period (722-481 B.C.) (she was one of the Four Beauties (四大美人) of Chinese history. They were Xi Shi of the Spring and Autumn Period, Wang Zhaojun of the Han Dynasty, Diao Chan of the Three kingdoms Period, and Yang Guifei of the Tang)
淡	dàn	lightly
妆	zhuāng	made up with cosmetics
濃	nóng	strong, heavily
抹	mǒ	to smear on, to apply heavily
淡妝濃抹		whether she is lightly made up or whether she is heavily made up (comparing her to the mist covering the scenery)
總	zǒng	always
相	xiāng	reciprocally, each other
相宜	yí	fits (her) very well

詩

惠崇＜春江曉景＞

竹外桃花三兩枝，
春江水暖鴨先知。
蔞蒿滿地蘆芽短，
正是河豚欲上時。

蘇軾
Sū Shì

∞

Su Shi came from a family with a history of government service. He spent a career as an official of the Northern Song and, although he frequently got into political conflicts and was even exiled, Su held high positions and served with distinction. He was part of the conservative faction that opposed the reformer Wang Anshi. Fortunately, Su Shi did not live to see the fall of the dynasty he served. He died in 1101, twenty-five years before the invasion of the barbarian hordes extinguished the Northern Song.

In his poetry Su makes frequent reference to foods–here fish, southwood, etc. He is thought to have been a gourmand *měi shí jiā* 美食家.

惠	Huì	person's name
崇	Chóng	person's name
惠崇		Hui Chong, a Buddhist monk and famous painter of the Northern Song Dynasty
春	chūn	spring
江	jiāng	river (here the Yangtze River)
曉	xiǎo	dawn
景	jǐng	scenery, scene, view
春江曉景		title of a painting by Hui Chong
竹	zhú	bamboo
外	wài	outside
桃	táo	peach, peach tree
花	huā	flower, blossom
三	sān	three
兩	liǎng	two
枝	zhī	branch, sprig

詩

春江	chūnjiāng	a "spring" river (Chinese poets write of spring rivers, autumn rivers, winter rivers, endowing the rivers with very different characteristics)
水	shuǐ	water
暖	nuǎn	warm
鴨	yā	duck
先	xiān	first, prior
知	zhī	know
春江水-暖鴨先知		this line is often quoted by the Chinese both in reference to the arrival of spring and to perspicacious people
蔞	lóu	a kind of Artemisia, an aromatic family of plants which includes sagebrush and wormwood
蒿	hāo	jungle, plants (this character is joined with other characters to produce proper names of plants)
蔞蒿		southernwood (it has edible stems)
滿	mǎn	full
地	dì	ground, earth
滿地		everywhere
蘆	lú	a reed
芽	yá	a sprout
短	duǎn	short

Continued ▶

正	zhèng	precise, true, correct, first, right
是	shì	to be
河	hé	river
豚	tún	globe fish, puffer fish
河豚		globe fish, puffer fish (a delicacy but poisonous if not properly prepared)
欲	yù	to want
上	shàng	above, on, to ascend (in China, the puffer fish swim upstream from the ocean to the Yangtze River in the springtime)
時	shí	time, season, time when…

詩

絕句

生當做人傑，死亦爲鬼雄。
至今思項羽，不肯過江東。

李清照
Lǐ Qīngzhào

∞

The poet is Li Qingzhao, China's most famous woman poet. She was from Jinan, the capital of Shandong, and her memorial hall, statue, library and inscriptions were established there. Born in the Song Dynasty, her life spanned the turbulent events of that time, from Kaifeng to Hangzhou.

Here it is possible that she exhorts the emperor that if he is going to live, be a hero; if he is going to die, be a ghost-hero. Remember the bravery of General Xiang Yu 項羽 (232–202 B.C.) who, defeated in his last battle, chose suicide rather than escape with dishonor.

There was little likelihood that the emperor would heed her call to heroic action. It was the cowardice of this very emperpor that led to the death of the patriot general Yue Fei. Moreover, if the emperor recovered north China, he would in the process liberate his father and older brother, both of whom were in line to succeed to the throne ahead of him.

Here Li Qingzhao has written a *jue ju* 絕句 (quatrain). She also wrote many poems in the *ci* style.

絕	jué	cut off, broken
句	jù	a sentence, a line
絕句		*jue ju*, a quatrain
生	shēng	alive
當	dāng	ought to
做	zuò	to be
人	rén	person
傑	jié	outstanding
人傑		hero, an outstanding person
死	sǐ	die
亦	yì	also
爲	wéi	to be
鬼	guǐ	spirit, ghost
雄	xióng	hero
鬼雄		spirit hero (when you're alive you want to be a hero in the living world, when you're dead you want to be a hero in the dead world)

詩

至	zhì	until, arrive at
今	jīn	now, present
思	sī	think, remind of, to miss
項	Xiàng	surname
羽	yǔ	feather, plume (here a person's name)
項羽		proper name (General Xiang Yu)
不	bù	no, not
肯	kěn	permit, be willing, agree
過	guò	pass through
江	jiāng	river
東	dōng	east (here the eastern bank of the Huai River where General Xiang Yu met defeat. The general was urged to flee but refused, saying "I brought eight thousand soldiers here, and they're all dead. I can't go home and face people")

病牛

耕犁千畝實千箱，
力盡筋疲誰復傷？
但得眾生皆得飽，
不辭羸病臥殘陽。

李綱
Lǐ Gāng

∞

Li Gang distinguished himself as a defender of the empire against the tatars. When they invaded, Li wrote a memorial in his own blood calling upon the emperor to abdicate. The emperor's son put Li Gang in command of the Chinese army which Li led in a successful defense of the capital. Emperor Gao Zong appointed Li Gang premier (*zaixiang*) but Li soon fell from power and lived out the remainer of his life in a Hangzhou monastery. It was an ignoble end for an ardent patriot.

This poem reflects Li's sacrifice.

詩

病	bìng	sick
牛	niú	cow, buffalo (this poem is told in the persona of the buffalo)
耕	gēng	to plow with a draft animal
犁	lí	to plow, a plow
千	qiān	a thousand, many
畝	mǔ	acre of land (Chinese measurement)
實	shí	to fill up
千	qiān	a thousand, many
箱	xiāng	container, storage bin (for grain)
力	lì	strength, force, power
盡	jìn	finish
筋	jīn	muscle
疲	pí	exhausted
誰	shuí	who
復	fù	again (here, be able to)
傷	shāng	wound, be wounded (who will feel wounded for you? Who will care about you?)
復傷		to sympathize with

Continued ▶

但	dàn	only
得	dé	able to, obtain
眾	zhòng	many
生	shēng	to produce, be born, life, living (here living creatures)
眾生		Buddhist concept (creator of mankind and creatures)
皆	jiē	all
得	dé	able to, obtain
飽	bǎo	to eat enough
不	bù	no, not
辭	cí	words, decline, be concerned, resign
不辭		(I) don't mind
羸	léi	thin, weak
病	bìng	illness, sickness
臥	wò	lie down
殘	cán	to injure, to destroy, incomplete, disabled
陽	yáng	sun
殘陽		setting sun

詩

曉出淨慈寺送林子方

畢竟西湖六月中，
風光不與四時同。
接天蓮葉無窮碧，
映日荷花別樣紅。

楊萬里
Yáng Wànlǐ

∞

Yang Wanli earned his *jinshi* degree in 1154 and became Keeper of the Imperial Library. He got into some trouble and was forced to take a provincial post for a while. Yang was a well known poet and wrote a very large number of poems in his lifetime.

This poem was written on the occasion of Yang's early morning trip to Jing Ci Temple to see off a Mr. Lin Zifang, although Mr. Lin's departure is not actually the subject of the poem.

This poem is frequently painted on paper fans.

曉	xiǎo	dawn, daybreak
出	chū	go out
淨	jìng	clean
慈	cí	loving mother
寺	sì	temple
淨慈寺		proper name (Jing Ci Temple)
送	sòng	send, send off
林	lín	forest (a Chinese surname)
子	zǐ	son, noun suffix (here used as a person's name)
方	fāng	square (here used as a person's name)
林子方		proper name (Lin Zifang)
畢	bì	to finish, conclude
竟	jìng	after all, in the end, finally
畢竟		after all, in the end, contrary to expectation (this phrase is still used today)
西	xī	west
湖	hú	lake
西湖		place name (West Lake in Hangzhou)
六	liù	six
月	yuè	month
中	zhōng	middle of the Lunar Calendar's June

詩

風	fēng	wind
光	guāng	light
風光		scenery
不	bù	no, not
與	yǔ	with
四	sì	four
時	shí	time, period, season
四時		the four seasons of the year
同	tóng	same
不與四-時同		the sixth month is different (不同 *bù tóng*) from the other seasons (actually, he implies that it is better than the others)
接	jiē	meet, like, merge, receive
天	tiān	sky, heaven
蓮	lián	lotus
葉	yè	leaf
無	wú	not have, doesn't
窮	qióng	end, finish
無窮		unending, continuous
碧	bì	green
接天蓮-葉無窮碧		the poet sees the green lotus leaves meeting the sky, merging into a continuous expanse of color

Continued ▶

映	yìng	relfect
日	rì	sun, day
荷	hé	lotus
花	huā	flower, blossom
別	bié	other, extra
樣	yàng	manner, kind, type
紅	hóng	red
別樣紅		the lotus flowers have an extraordinary red color

小池

泉眼無聲惜細流，
樹陰照水愛晴柔。
小荷才露尖尖角，
早有蜻蜓立上頭。

楊萬里
Yáng Wànlǐ

∞

Yang Wanli served as an official in Shao Xing, among other places, and received numerous promotions to high office. Yang ran into some difficulty when he was pressured to write a good recommendation for an unsavory official named Han Tuozhou 傅伯壽. Yang refused to recommend the man. The emperor offered Yang a higher office if he would write the recommendation, but Yang stood on principle and refused. Nevertheless Han rose in favor and Yang's career declined. At age 83 Yang Wanli talked to his family about Han, broke down and wept. He asked for paper, wrote down Han's crimes, wrote a farewell poem to his wife and children, threw away the pen, and died.

Yang Wanli wrote many lovely pastoral poems (*tianyuan shi* 田園詩) but this is his most famous. The Chinese often quote the line in which the dragonfly stands on its head as a metaphor for people just beginning to show their capacities.

小	xiǎo	small
池	chí	pond, pool
泉	quán	a spring
眼	yǎn	eye
泉眼		hole where a spring flows out
無	wú	have not, does not
聲	shēng	noise, sound, voice
惜	xī	lovely, to consider lovely, to cherish, to treasure
細	xì	fine, delicate, thin
流	liú	flow
樹	shù	tree
陰	yīn	shade
照	zhào	shine, reflect, photograph
水	shuǐ	water
愛	ài	to like
晴	qíng	clear (weather), fair (weather)
柔	róu	gentle, soft

詩

小	xiǎo	small
荷	hé	lotus leaves
才	cái	just now, only then, talent
露	lù	expose
尖尖	jiān	tapering, pointed, sharply pointed (the leaves of the lotus are sharply pointed)
角	jiǎo	corner, angle, horn
早	zǎo	early
有	yǒu	exist, to have
蜻	qīng	dragonfly
蜓	tíng	dragonfly
蜻蜓		a dragonfly
立	lì	to stand
上	shàng	above, on, to ascend
頭	tóu	head

示兒

死去元知萬事空，
但悲不見九州同。
王師北定中原日，
家祭無忘告乃翁。

陸游
Lù Yóu

Lu You is remembered as a patriot of the Southern Song Dynasty. He fought as a general against the barbarian Jin Dynasty and remained a life-long opponent of appeasement. He would not accept a position under the Jin. Lu was a member of a patriotic faction that continued to agitate for armed defense of China, causing them to be political outcasts.

詩

示	shì	to display, to show (here to instruct)
兒	ér	child
死	sǐ	die
去	qù	depart
死去		to die
元	yuán	originally
知	zhī	know
萬	wàn	ten thousand
事	shì	things, matters
空	kōng	empty
但	dàn	but
悲	bēi	sad
不	bú	no, not
見	jiàn	see, perceive
九	jiǔ	nine
州	zhōu	an administrative geographical area
九州		China
同	tóng	together (here united)

Continued ▶

王	wáng	king, imperial
師	shī	an army
北	běi	north
定	dìng	to settle, to fix (here to have captured)
中	zhōng	middle, in, within
原	yuán	a plain, prairie
中原		China's Central Plain (the area of modern Henan and Anhui Provinces)
日	rì	sun, day
家	jiā	home, family, establishment
祭	jì	to sacrifice, memorial ceremony
家祭		sacrifice to ancestors
無	wú	not
忘	wàng	forget
告	gào	tell
乃	nǎi	your, possessive pronoun
翁	wēng	elderly man (title of respect for father)

詩

秋夜將曉,
出籬門迎涼有感

三萬里河東入海,
五千仞岳上摩天。
遺民淚盡胡塵里,
南望王師又一年。

陸游
Lù Yóu

∞

Lu You was an ardent patriot and a poet with an enormous literary output. The most prolific writer of Chinese poetry in history was the Qianlong Emperor (1711-1799). The second most prolific was Lu You, of whom more than nine thousand poems survive.

According to Lu, those who refuse to serve under the Jin Tatars weep under foreign occupation. They look southward one more year and wait for the Chinese army to come.

Lu was in the south but was thinking of Chinese in the north, under occupation by the Jin Dynasty.

秋	qiū	autumn
夜	yè	night
將	jiāng	nearly
曉	xiǎo	dawn
出	chū	come out, go out
籬	lí	a fence of bamboo or wattle
門	mén	door, gate
迎	yíng	to welcome, to meet, to receive
涼	liáng	cool
有	yǒu	to exist, to have
感	gǎn	to influence, to move, to affect
有感		to inspire
三	sān	three
萬	wàn	ten thousand
里	lǐ	mile (a Chinese mile is equivalent to one-third of a modern English mile)
河	hé	river (here the Yellow River)
東	dōng	east
入	rù	enter
海	hǎi	sea

詩

五	wǔ	five
千	qiān	thousand
仞	rèn	length measure word for eight feet
岳	yuè	moutain peak (here refers to Hua Mountain)
上	shàng	above, on, to ascend
摩	mó	to touch
天	tiān	heaven, sky
遺	yí	to bequeath, leave behind
民	mín	people
遺民		those who refuse to accept office under a new dynasty
淚	lèi	tears, to weep
盡	jìn	exhaust, exhaustively
胡	hú	Tatar peoples
塵	chén	dust
胡塵		clouds of dust raised by the horses of the invading Tatars
里	lǐ	inside

Continued ▶

南	nán	south
望	wàng	to look
王	wáng	kind, royal
師	shī	military, army
又	yòu	again
一	yì	a, one
年	nián	year

游山西村

莫笑農家臘酒渾，
豐年留客足雞豚。
山重水復疑無路，
柳暗花明又一村。

陸游
Lù Yóu

The Song Dynasty had a much smaller poetic output than the Tang. There were basically two major poets; Su Shi and Lu You. Lu was over eighty when he wrote this poem, during a time when he used to visit his friend in a village near Shao Xing. Here he advises us not to despise the cloudy wine served in country homes. When the peasants have a bumper harvest they will invite you in for a sumptous feast.

The last two lines of this poem are often quoted to give someone encouragement. Just when you are about to give up, you see that there is hope. When you're unsure of the way and you must cross mountains and streams, you'll suddenly discover the road to your village.

The Shanxi mentioned is in Zhejiang Province, not modern Shanxi Province. The name of the town is Shao Xing. Lu You, Lu Xun and Zhou Enlai all came from Shao Xing.

游	yóu	enjoy, to enjoy oneself, tour, travel (in modern Chinese 遊覽 *yóu lǎn*)
山	shān	mountain
西	xī	west
山西		place name
村	cūn	village
莫	mò	do not
笑	xiào	laugh at
農	nóng	agriculture, agricultural, rustic
家	jiā	house, family, establishment
臘	là	last month of a lunar calendar (wine made during that month is called 臘酒 *là jiǔ*. It is good quality wine owing to exposure to cold weather)
酒	jiǔ	wine
渾	hún	murky, cloudy (their *là jiǔ* wine is cloudy, therefore not very good)
豐	fēng	abundant, rich
年	nián	year (here it means their annual harvest)
留	liú	to stay, to be invited to stay (here the locals will invite you to stay and will serve you a meal)
客	kè	guest
足	zú	enough
雞	jī	chicken
豚	tún	pork

詩

山	shān	mountain
重	chóng	again, repeatedly (here it means many)
水	shuǐ	water, river
復	fù	again (here mountain after mountain and river after river, row after row of mountains, etc.)
疑	yí	doubt
無	wú	not have
路	lù	road
柳	liǔ	willow
暗	àn	dark
花	huā	flower
明	míng	bright
又	yòu	again, again and again
一	yì	one
村	cūn	village

四時田園雜興

畫出耘田夜績麻，
村莊兒女各當家。
童孫未解供耕織，
也傍桑陰學種瓜。

范成大
Fàn Chéngdà

∞

Fan Chengda had a brilliant career. While young he was promoted to very high office. The appointment caused such a furor among the bureaucrats that the emperor had to demote him to a lower office to placate critics. Fan served as magistrate, as envoy to the Tatars, and as defense attache to Sichuan. He eventually became Minister of State.

Fan wrote records of his travels, a large treatise on chrysanthemums and a collection of ci poems. He is a well-known writer of pastoral poems (*tianyuan shi* 田園诗). Here Fan proclaims the mixed pleasures of field and garden, as the children learn to plant melons.

詩

四	sì	four
時	shí	time, season
田	tián	field
園	yuán	garden
雜	zá	mixed, miscellaneous
興	xìng	pleasure, interest
晝	zhòu	daytime
出	chū	come out, go out
耘	yún	to weed, to hoe
田	tián	field
夜	yè	night
績	jī	to spin threads
麻	má	hemp, flax
村	cūn	village
莊	zhuāng	village
村莊		village
兒	ér	man
女	nǚ	woman
各	gè	each
當	dāng	hold a position, ought to
家	jiā	home, family, establishment
當家		occupy a position as head of the household

Continued ▶

童	tóng	child
孫	sūn	grandchild
未	wèi	not yet
解	jiě	understand
供	gōng	to offer, offering
耕	gēng	to plow
織	zhī	to weave
也	yě	also, and, even
傍	bàng	near
桑	sāng	mulberry tree
陰	yīn	shade
學	xué	learn
種	zhòng	to plant
瓜	guā	melon

詩

觀書有感

半畝方塘一鑒開，
天光雲影共徘徊。
問渠那得清如許，
爲有源頭活水來。

朱熹
Zhū Xī

∞

Zhu Xi was one of the most remarkable men in Chinese history—a philosopher who single-handedly changed the interpretation of Confucianism. Beginning in the second half of the twelfth century, his numerous writings popularized a revised approach to the Classics based on the mixed influences of Daoism and Buddhism. Zhu Xi's school, Neo-Confucianism, came to dominate education and changed Chinese society.

In this poem scholarship is seen to depend on one's supply of knowledge (spring) from books (pond). Water needs to be freshly supplied or it will become stagnant. The Chinese say there is moving water (*huó shuî* 活水), and stagnant water (*sî shuî* 死水). Pond water ought to be circulating.

觀	guān	look, see, watch, observe
書	shū	to write, writing, book
有	yǒu	to have, exist
感	gǎn	feeling, opinion
半	bàn	half
畝	mǔ	Chinese acre, measurement of land
方	fāng	square
塘	táng	pool, pond
一	yí	a, one
鑒	jiàn	mirror
開	kāi	open (here remove the cover from the mirror. Chinese mirrors have dust covers)
天	tiān	sky, heaven
光	guāng	light
雲	yún	cloud
影	yǐng	shadow
共	gòng	together
徘	pái	to pace, hesitate
徊	huái	to pace
徘徊		to pace up and down, to stroll

詩

問	wèn	ask
渠	qú	ditch, pond
那	nǎ	where, how
得	dé	obtain, achieve
清	qīng	clean
如	rú	like, as
許	xǔ	praise, promise, allow, surname (here, "this, that")
如許		like that
爲	wèi	because of, due to
有	yǒu	to have, exist
源	yuán	origin
頭	tóu	head
源頭		origin
活	huó	alive, lively, moving
水	shuǐ	water
來	lái	come (refers to spring which provides fresh water)

湖上

花開紅樹亂鶯啼，
草長平湖白鷺飛。
風日晴和人意好，
夕陽簫鼓几船歸。

徐元傑
Xú Yuánjié

∞

Xu Yuanjie got his *jinshi* degree about AD. 1230 and served in a number of posts. He acquired a reputation for sensitive dealings with subordinates, preferring always to convince people by logical persuasion rather than autocratic methods. The population under his authority were reputed to be very happy. Xu admonished the emperor and gave lessons to the emperor in governing. The emperor was said to have made inspection tours throughout the empire, feeling secure because he was relying on Xu's advice.

An evil official, Shi Songzhi, was employed by the emperor. Xu Yuanjie put an end to Shi's nefarious conduct. Afterwards, while speaking to the emperor, Xu suddenly collapsed and died in agony. Friends and supporters suspected that Shi had poisoned Xu. They demanded a full investigation, but the investigation produced no conclusive results. The emperor grieved over Xu's death.

The lake in the poem is, as usual, West Lake in Hangzhou. A *xiao* 簫 is a long bamboo flute, played vertically like a clarinet.

詩

湖	hú	lake
上	shàng	above, on, to ascend
花	huā	flower, blossom
開	kāi	to open
紅	hóng	red
樹	shù	tree
亂	luàn	confusion, in confusion
鶯	yīng	oriole
啼	tí	sing, sound made by a bird
草	cǎo	grass
長	zhǎng	grow
平	píng	even, level, tranquil, flat
湖	hú	lake
白	bái	white
鷺	lù	the egret
飛	fēi	to fly

Continued ▶

風	fēng	wind
日	rì	day, sun
風日		scenery
晴	qíng	bright, sunny
和	hé	peace, peaceful, harmonious
人	rén	person
意	yì	idea, feeling, mood
好	hǎo	good
夕	xī	evening
陽	yáng	sun
夕陽		setting sun
簫	xiāo	flute, the long bamboo flute, held vertically like a clarinet
鼓	gǔ	drum
幾	jǐ	several, how many
船	chuán	boat
歸	guī	return

詩

橫溪堂春曉

一把青秧趁手青，
輕煙漠漠雨冥冥。
東風染盡三千頃，
白鷺飛來無處停。

虞似良
Yú Sìliáng

∞

The Song Dynasty poet Yu Siliang is not famous. Yu named himself *Bao Lian Shan Ren*, the Man of the Bao Lian Mountains, out of admiration for his favorite mountain range. Yu is known for his expertise in Official Style (*Li Shu*) calligraphy and is the author of the *Zhuan Li Yun Shu*, or, in English, the Rhyming Book of Seal Style and Official Style Calligraphy.

The egret, an elegant and noble image in Chinese poetry, always refers to a recluse.

橫	héng	horizontal
溪	xī	stream
堂	táng	building, a reception room
橫溪堂		name of a building in Zhejiang Province (the ruins of the building may still be seen)
春	chūn	spring
曉	xiǎo	dawn, daybreak
一	yì	a, one
把	bǎ	to take, to grasp, measure word for a bunch
青	qīng	green
秧	yāng	rice seedling
趁	chèn	take advantage of, avail oneself of, follow
手	shǒu	hand (here the rice seedling avails itself of my hand (by my planting it) and becomes green)
青	qīng	green
輕	qīng	light in weight
煙	yān	smoke
漠漠	mò	misty
雨	yǔ	rain
冥冥	míng míng	dark, obscure

詩

東	dōng	east
風	fēng	wind
染	rǎn	to dye
盡	jìn	to exhaust, to the utmost
三	sān	three
千	qiān	a thousand
頃	qǐng	100 Chinese acres
白	bái	white
鷺	lù	an egret
飛	fēi	fly
來	lái	come
無	wú	haven't, doesn't
處	chù	place
停	tíng	stop (there's no place to alight. There are green seedlings everywhere)

樵夫

一擔干柴古渡頭，
盤纏一日頗優游。
歸來澗底磨刀斧，
又作全家明日謀。

蕭德藻
Xiāo Dézǎo

∞

The obscure poet Xiao Dezao watches a gatherer of firewood scavenge at a deserted ferryboat landing. The profit from this menial labor is so small that it is adequate for the family for only one day.

詩

樵	qiáo	fuel, to gather fuel
夫	fū	person, laborer, artisan
一	yí	one, a
擔	dàn	bunch
干	gān	dry, dried
柴	chái	firewood
古	gǔ	ancient
渡	dù	to cross over, to ferry, a ferry
頭	tóu	the head, the top
渡頭		a ferry slip, a ferry crossing
盤	pán	dish, examine, coil up, expenses, costs
纏	chán	wrap up
盤纏		payment (here travelling money)
一	yí	one, a
日	rì	sun, day
頗	pō	quite, rather
優	yōu	abundant, excellent
游	yóu	swim, float
優游		leisurely and carefree (life), ample

Continued ▶

歸	guī	to return
來	lái	come
澗	jiàn	valley, gorge
底	dǐ	bottom
磨	mó	to rub (here to sharpen)
刀	dāo	knife
斧	fǔ	axe
又	yòu	again
作	zuò	make, do
全	quán	whole, entire
家	jiā	home, family, establishment
全家		the whole family
明	míng	bright
明日		tomorrow
謀	móu	a plan, a device (here to make a living)

詩

游園不值

應憐屐齒印蒼苔，
小扣柴扉久不開。
春色滿園關不住，
一枝紅杏出牆來。

葉紹翁
Yè Shàowēng

∞

The Song Dynasty poet Ye Shaoweng is a shadowy figure. We don't know his dates of birth or death and know little of his career.

Ye's grandfather was demoted and thus his career to serve in office was affected by his family's history. For a short time he held a small official title. For most of his life, he lived in seclusion near by the Qiantang West lake. He is remembered only for this poem.

The poet is afraid his clogs will crush the cultivated moss lawn. Athough he does not go into the garden, a bough of apricot blossoms hangs out over the garden wall.

游	yóu	to play, to visit
園	yuán	garden, park
不	bù	no, not
值	zhí	meet, succeed, worth, price
不值		to fail, not come to fruition, attain no result
應	yīng	maybe, perhaps
憐	lián	to pity, sympathize
屐	jī	clogs, wooden footwear
齒	chǐ	serrations, teeth, corrugations
印	yìn	to stamp, to imprint
蒼	cāng	dark green
苔	tái	moss
蒼苔		moss
小	xiǎo	little, small
扣	kòu	knock (on door)
柴	chái	wooden
扉	fēi	door
久	jiǔ	long time
不	bù	no, not
開	kāi	open (perhaps it is because the man is afraid the poet will crush his cultivated moss lawn)

詩

春	chūn	spring
色	sè	color
滿	mǎn	fill, full
園	yuán	garden, park
關	guān	close, to shut up
不	bú	no, not
住	zhù	reside, stop, auxiliary verb indicating completed action
關不住		cannot close
一	yì	a, one
枝	zhī	stem, branch, a measure word
紅	hóng	red
杏	xìng	apricot (a red apricot blossom)
出	chū	come out, go out
牆	qiáng	wall
來	lái	come

江村晚眺

江頭落日照平沙，
潮退漁船擱岸斜。
白鳥一雙臨水立，
見人驚起入蘆花。

戴復古
Dài Fùgǔ

∞

Dai Fugu is credited with having advanced the art of poetry to such an extent that he is compared with the great Meng Haoran in compositional technique. The Chinese revere him for his style.

Dai traveled for over twenty years visiting China's famous places. He was a poet of the Southern Song.

詩

江村晚眺	jiāng	river
	cūn	village
	wǎn	evening
	tiào	to peer into the distance from a high place
江頭落日照平沙	jiāng	river
	tóu	head (here a bend in the river)
	luò	to fall, drop, let drop
	rì	sun, day
	zhào	shine
	píng	level, even
	shā	sand
潮退漁船	cháo	tide
	tuì	recede
	yú	fish
	chuán	boat
漁船		fishing boat
擱岸斜	gē	to put, place
	àn	shore, bank
	xiá	slanting, tilted, inclined

Continued ▶

白	bái	white
鳥	niǎo	bird
一	yì	one, a
雙	shuāng	pair
臨	lín	to face, be near to
水	shuǐ	water
立	lì	to stand
見	jiàn	to see, perceive
人	rén	person
驚	jīng	surprised, shock
起	qǐ	arise
入	rù	enter
蘆	lú	reed, rush
花	huā	flower, blossom
蘆花		cattails, water plants

詩

題臨安邸

山外青山樓外樓，
西湖歌舞几時休？
暖風熏得游人醉，
直把杭州作汴州。

林升
Lín Shēng

Lin Sheng was a poet of the South Song. He is not famous. To quote this poem to someone implies that there are capable people other than you. There are mountains better than this mountain, there are buildings better than this building, etc.

He asks, when will all the singing and dancing end? In the north, Kaifeng had been taken by the barbarian Jin Dynasty. By comparing it to Hangzhou, Lin Sheng is criticizing the court. The emperor in Hangzhou isn't calling on the people to recapture Kaifeng. In Hangzhou they merely sing and dance.

題	tí	the forehead (thus a heading, an inscription, an inscribed poem)
臨	lín	near to, come to
安	ān	peace, tranquility
臨安		place, name (the old name for Hangzhou)
邸	dǐ	the house of an official
山	shān	mountain
外	wài	outside
青	qīng	green
山	shān	mountain
樓	lóu	multi-storied building
外	wài	outside
樓	lóu	multi-storied building
西	xī	west
湖	hú	lake
西湖		place name (West Lake in Hangzhou)
歌	gē	song
舞	wǔ	dance
几	jǐ	several, how many, how much
時	shí	time, season
几時		when
休	xiū	to rest (here to finish)

詩

暖	nuǎn	warm (of weather)
風	fēng	wind
熏	xūn	smoke, fog
得	dé	obtain
游	yóu	travel, visit
人	rén	person
游人		visitor, traveler
醉	zuì	intoxicated
直	zhí	straight, upright, only, merely
把	bǎ	to take (it precedes the object)
杭	háng	a barge
州	zhōu	an administrative geographical region
杭州		place name (Hangzhou in Zhejiang Province. The capital of the Southern Song dynasty)
作	zuò	make, do, act (here to act in the capacity of… To take Hangzhou to be Bianzhou)
汴	biàn	proper name (name of an ancient river in Henan)
州	zhōu	an administrative geographical region
汴州		place name (old name for Kaifeng in Henan Province. Capital of the Northern Song Dynasty)

月子彎彎照九州

月子彎彎照九州，
几家歡樂几家愁！
几家高樓飲美酒，
几家飄流在外頭。

無名氏
Anonymous

∞

This anonymous folksong, like folksongs everywhere, complains of social problems.

In China a crescent moon has ominous connotations. Something will soon end. By contrast, a full moon has cheerful connotations, such as being the occasion for the family reunion dinner (*tuan yuan* 團圓).

詩

月	yuè	moon, month
子	zǐ	noun suffix
月子		moon
彎彎	wān	curved (here crescent)
照	zhào	shine
九	jiǔ	nine
州	zhōu	region
九州		China (in antiquity Yu The Great divided China into nine regions)
月	yuè	moon, month
子	zǐ	noun suffix
月子		moon
彎彎	wān	curved (here crescent)
照	zhào	shine
九	jiǔ	nine
州	zhōu	region
九州		China (in antiquity Yu The Great divided China into nine regions)

Continued ▶

幾	jǐ	several, how many
家	jiā	home, family, establishment
歡	huān	pleased, to be glad
樂	lè	happy
歡樂		happy
幾	jǐ	several, how many
家	jiā	home, family, establishment
愁	chóu	anxious, grieving
幾	jǐ	several, how many
家	jiā	home, family, establishment
高	gāo	tall, high
樓	lóu	milti-storied building (to drink in a high building implies wealth. Only a rich person would live in a multi-storied house)
飲	yǐn	to drink
美	měi	beautiful (here delicious)
酒	jiǔ	wine

詩

几	jǐ	several, how many
家	jiā	home, family, establishment
飄	piāo	to whirl in the wind
流	liú	to flow
飄流		to drift about
在	zài	at, in, on
外	wài	out, outside
頭	tóu	noun suffix, head, top
外頭		outside (outside of their homes. Homeless, vagrants)

天淨沙
（秋思）

枯藤老樹昏鴉，
小橋流水人家，
古道西風瘦馬。
夕陽西下，斷腸人在天涯。

馬致遠
Mǎ Zhìyuǎn

∞

Ma Zhiyuan describes this poem as belonging to the genre Autumn Reveries (*qiusi* 秋思). He also specifies that the poem is to be sung to the tune "Sky of Clean Sand". Yuan Dynasty tunes (*pai*) were well established, and poets set words to them. This poem is a type of *qu* called a *xiaoling* (*qiusi* 小令), a short *qu*. Notice that the poem has only two verbs, *xia* 下 in line four and *zai* 在 in line five. All other words are nouns.

詩

天	tiān	sky, heaven
淨	jìng	clean
沙	shā	sand
秋	qiū	autumn
思	sī	think, thought, reflect, reverie, meditation
枯	kū	to wither, dry up
藤	téng	wine
老	lǎo	old
樹	shù	tree
昏	hūn	dusk, evening
鴉	yā	crow, raven
小	xiǎo	small
橋	qiáo	bridge
流	liú	flow
水	shuǐ	water
人	rén	a person, person's
家	jiā	home, house, family, establishment

Continued ▶

古	gǔ	old
道	dào	road, lane
西	xī	west
風	fēng	wind
西風		a west wind implies an autumn wind
瘦	shòu	thin
馬	mǎ	horse
夕	xī	evening
陽	yáng	sun
西	xī	west
下	xiá	beneath, under, to descend
斷	duàn	to break
腸	cháng	intestines, entrails
斷腸		conventional poetic phrase meaning to break one's heart, heartbreaking
人	rén	a person, person's
在	zài	at, in, on
天	tiān	sky, heaven
涯	yá	side, edge, margin, limit
天涯		at the edge of the sky, on the distant horizon (according to Chinese mythology, Pan Gu split the heavens with an axe. Traditional Chinese viewed the sky as a large plane having edges at the horizon. To be at the far edge of the sky meant to be very far away)

詩

田舍夜舂

新婦舂糧獨睡遲，
夜寒茅屋雨來時。
燈前每囑兒休哭，
明日行人要早炊。

高啟
Gāo Qǐ

Gao Qi wrote melancholy poems, full of sympathy and regret. This poem, set in a time of war, reveals the drudgery and loneliness of a young wife.

田	tián	field, if an adjective—rustic, country
舍	shè	cottage, shed
田舍		peasant's house
夜	yè	night
舂	chōng	to pound, to pestle, to grind grain (here the sound of grinding grain)
新	xīn	new
婦	fù	woman
新婦		young wife
舂	chōng	to pound, to pestle, to grind grain (here the sound of grinding grain)
糧	liáng	grain
獨	dú	single, only, alone
睡	shuì	sleep
遲	chí	late (it is late but she is still up grinding grain)
夜	yè	night
寒	hán	cold
茅	máo	woven grass mat
屋	wū	room, house
茅屋		thatched cottage
雨	yǔ	rain
來	lái	come
時	shí	time, at the time of…

詩

燈	dēng	lantern, lamp, light
前	qián	before, in front of
每	měi	each, every, every time (here several times)
囑	zhǔ	to enjoin, advise, urge
兒	ér	child
休	xiū	to rest, desist, do not…
哭	kū	cry
明	míng	bright
日	rì	sun, day
明日		tomorrow
行	xíng	go
人	rén	person
行人		the person who is going out (presumably her husband)
要	yào	want, need
早	zǎo	early
炊	cuī	to cook a meal

詠石灰

千錘萬鑿出深山，
烈火焚燒若等閑；
粉骨碎身渾不怕，
要留清白在人間！

于謙
Yú Qiān

∞

Yu Qian compares himself to whitewash (limestone). Lime may be hammered and chiseled out of the mountains, fired and diluted with water to make whitewash, but it remains white (pure). Yu Qian remained pure (loyal). When the Mongols attacked Beijing and captured the emperor, Yu Qian, serving as Ming Dynasty Commander-in Chief, rejected appeasement. He defended the capital and defeated the Mongols.

Unfortunately Yu Qian supported the emperor's successor. When the captive emperor was restored, he thought Yu Qian had betrayed him and had Yu executed.

詩

詠	yǒng	to praise, in praise of…
石	shí	rock, stone
灰	huī	ash
石灰		whitewash, limestone
千	qiān	thousand
錘	chuí	a hammer blow, strike of a hammer
萬	wàn	ten thousand
鑿	záo	chisel
出	chū	go out, come out
深	shēn	deep
山	shān	mountain, hill
烈	liè	strong, fierce
火	huǒ	fire
焚	fén	to burn
燒	shāo	to burn
若	ruò	like, as
等	děng	grade, rank, wait, and so forth
閑	xián	idle, unoccupied, leisure
等閑		ordinary, unimportant

Continued ▶

粉	fěn	powder
骨	gǔ	bones
碎	suì	break, pulverize
身	shēn	body
粉骨碎身		a conventional four-character phrase similar to "go through heaven and hell"
渾	hún	all, whole, unsophisticated
不	bú	no, not
怕	pà	to fear
要	yào	want
留	liú	keep
清	qīng	clean
白	bái	white
清白		a person free from any wrongdoing
在	zài	at, in, on
人	rén	person
間	jiān	between, among
人間		among people, in the world

詩

由商丘入永城途中作

三月輕風麥浪生，
黃河岸上晚波平。
村原處處垂楊柳，
一路青青到永城。

李先芳
Lǐ Xiānfāng

Li Xianfang received his *jinshi* degree in the mid-1500's, toward the end of the Ming. Not much is known about his performance in the offices he held. Li wrote prolifically and put together three collections of his own poetry.

由	yóu	from
商	shāng	to discuss, commerce
丘	qiū	mound, grave
商丘		place name (in Henan Provnice)
入	rù	enter
永	yǒng	perpetual, perpetually
城	chéng	city
永城		place name (in Henan Provnice)
途	tú	road
中	zhōng	middle, in, within
作	zuò	do, act, write (here, written on the road…)
三	sān	three, third
月	yuè	month
輕	qīng	light in weight
風	fēng	wind
麥	mài	wheat
浪	làng	a wave
生	shēng	produce, be born, life, living (here produce waves)

詩

黃	huáng	yellow
河	hé	river
黃河		place name (Yellow River)
岸	àn	bank, shore
上	shàng	above, on, to ascend
晚	wǎn	evening
波	bō	wave, ripple
平	píng	even, level, tranquil, flat
村	cūn	village
原	yuán	a plain, a prairie (here the plain outside the village)
處	chù	place
處處		everyplace
垂	chuí	to droop, to hang down
楊	yáng	poplar tree
柳	liǔ	willow tree
一	yí	one
路	lù	road
一路		along the road
青青	qīng qīng	green, verdant
到	dào	arrive at
永	yǒng	perpetual, perpetually
城	chéng	city

軍中夜感

慘淡天昏與地荒，
西風殘月冷沙場。
裹屍馬革英雄事，
縱死終令汗竹香。

張家玉
Zhāng Jiāyù

∞

Zhang Jiayu was a southerner, a good poet, but not very famous. He got his *jinshi* degree about 1643 and held a succession of offices. Eventually fate led him into the political turbulence and violence that occurred at the end of the Ming. Zhang possessed great devotion to duty. When his soldiers lost a battle with rebels, he flung himself into a river and drowned.

The deeds of heroes are written in history books which, in ancient China, were made of bamboo strips. To harden the bamboo and make it insect-proof, the bamboo was fired, which made it sweat. Thus even though you die, you emit a frangrance of sweating bamboo.

Only the body of someone important, like a hero, would be wrapped in horsehide and sent back to China for burial.

詩

軍	jūn	army, military
中	zhōng	middle, in, within (here in the military)
夜	yè	night
感	gǎn	feeling, to feel (here the feeling you're going to be killed)
慘	cǎn	sorrowful
淡	dàn	insipid, pale, weak
慘淡		gloomy, bleak, dismal
天	tiān	heaven, sky
昏	hūn	dusk, dark
與	yǔ	and, with
地	dì	place, ground, earth
荒	huāng	wild, barren
天昏與地荒		a conventional five-character phrase meaning a smoky sky over a dark earth, dark all around
西	xī	west
風	fēng	wind
殘	cán	curved, crescent
月	yuè	moon, month
冷	lěng	cold, to chill
沙	shā	sand, sandy
場	chǎng	ground
沙場		a battlefield

Continued ▶

裹	guǒ	to bind, wrap
屍	shī	corpse
馬	mǎ	horse
革	gé	leather, hide
英	yīng	flower, hero
雄	xióng	male, grand, powerful, hero
英雄		hero
事	shì	matter, affair
縱	zòng	even if, even though
死	sǐ	die
終	zhōng	finally
令	lìng	to cause
汗	hàn	perspire, sweat
竹	zhú	bamboo
汗竹		historical record (either of the compounds *hanzhu* (to sweat out the bamboo) or *hanqing* 汗青 (to sweat out the green) can mean historical record)
香	xiāng	fragrant

貞溪初夏

棟花風起漾微波，
野渡舟橫客自過。
沙上兒童臨水立，
戲將萍葉飼新鵝。

邵亨貞
Shào Hēngzhēn

Shao Hengzhen is not famous. He was from Yan Ling, served in the minor position of Sub-director of Learning in *Songjiang* 棟 Prefecture, lived to be ninety-three years old.

貞	zhēn	true, loyal, faithful, staunch
溪	xī	stream
貞溪		place name (Zhen Creek in Songjiang County, Shanghai)
初	chū	first, early
夏	xià	summer
楝	liàn	chinaberry tree
花	huā	flower, blossom
風	fēng	summer breeze
起	qǐ	arise
漾	yàng	undulate, ripple
微	wēi	tiny, small
波	bō	wave, ripple
野	yě	wild, the wilds
渡	dù	ferry
野渡		a rustic ford, ferry crossing, ferry slip
舟	zhōu	boat
橫	héng	crosswise, horizontal (here the boat is bobbing crosswise while tied up)
客	kè	guest
自	zì	self
過	guò	to pass

詩

沙	shā	sand
上	shàng	above, on, to ascend
兒	ér	child
童	tóng	child
兒童		children
臨	lín	to face, overlook, near, nearly
水	shuǐ	water
立	lì	to stand
戲	xì	to have fun, to play with
將	jiāng	to take, to grasp
萍	píng	duckweed
葉	yè	leaf
飼	sì	to feed, to nourish
新	xīn	new (here young)
鵝	é	baby goose

雜詩

九州生氣恃風雷，
萬馬齊喑究可哀。
我勸天公重抖擻，
不拘一格降人才。

龔自珍
Gōng Zìzhēn

Gong Zizhen is famous. Born late in the Qing Dynasty in Hangzhou (then called Ren He 仁和), he received his *jinshi* degree in 1829. Intelligent and talented, Gong had a distinctly antiquarian temperment. As an official in the Board of Rites he specialized in the Gong Yang branch of the Spring and Autumn Annals, He was also an expert on the geography of China's northwest border. Although Gong was influenced by Zhou culture and the Spring and Autumn Annals he employed an independent style of composition. His prose is seen as mysterious and profound; his poetry beautiful. The *Ding An Quan Ji* 定庵全集 collection of his poems is named after his hao name Gong Ding'an.

This is a political poem (*zheng zhi shi* 政治詩). Gong is telling the emperor that the emperor is not alone. There are other people of talent that can be used.

詩

雜	zá	miscellaneous
詩	shī	poem
九	jiǔ	nine
州	zhōu	a geographical region
九州		the Nine Regions (another name for China)
生	shēng	to produce, be born, life, living
氣	qì	air, energy
生氣		vitality
恃	shì	depend on
風	fēng	wind
雷	léi	thunder
風雷		wind and thunder mean social reform
萬	wàn	ten thousand
馬	mǎ	horse (the ten thousand horses refer to the people who want to reform society)
齊	qí	together
喑	yīn	silent, mute
究	jiū	outcome, actually, after all
可	kě	can
哀	āi	make people feel very sad or pathetic

Continued ▶

我	wǒ	I
勸	quàn	to persuade, exhort, advise
天	tiān	heaven, sky
公	gōng	duke, male, open, public
天公		ruler of nature
重	chóng	again, to repeat (if pronounced *zhòng* it means heavy, important)
抖	dǒu	shake, rouse
擻	sǒu	shake, poke
抖擻		to shake up, pull oneself together, make an effort
不	bù	no, not
拘	jū	to grasp, adhere to
一	yì	a, one
格	gé	standard, specification, format, pattern, style
降	jiàng	descend (here to use, the emperor deigns to use)
人	rén	person
才	cái	talent, genius, then
人才		talent, genius, elites (Gong Zizhen is referring to the talent of the reformers)

明日

明日復明日，明日何其多！
我生待明日，萬事成蹉跎。

無名氏
Anonymous

This Anonymous poem could come from any age. Every Chinese child knows it by heart. Parents recite this poem to children who procrastinate.

明	míng	bright
日	rì	sun, day
明日		tomorrow
明日		bright, sun, day, tomorrow
復	fù	again
明日		bright, sun, day, tomorrow
明日		bright, sun, day, tomorrow
何	hé	how
其	qí	emphatic particle, this, that, his, her, its
何其		how, how much, how many tomorrow…
多	duō	many
我	wǒ	I
生	shēng	produce, be born, life, living
待	dài	wait
明日		bright, sun, day, tomorrow
萬	wàn	ten thousand
事	shì	matter, affair, things
成	chéng	complete
蹉	cuō	to slip, to pass by, fall off
跎	tuó	to slip, to pass by, fall off
蹉跎		to let time slip by, to idle away time

Made in United States
Orlando, FL
16 April 2024